Psychoanalysis and Repetition

SUNY series in Contemporary French Thought

—————————

David Pettigrew and François Raffoul, editors

Psychoanalysis and Repetition

Why Do We Keep Making the Same Mistakes?

Juan-David Nasio

Translated by

David Pettigrew

SUNY
PRESS

Published by State University of New York Press, Albany

L'Inconscient, c'est la répétition! © 2012, Éditions Payot & Rivages

© 2019 State University of New York

For information, contact State University of New York Press, Albany, NY
www.sunypress.edu

Library of Congress Cataloging-in-Publication Data

Names: Nasio, Juan-David, author. | Pettigrew, David, 1951– translator.
Title: Psychoanalysis and repetition : why do we keep making the same
  mistakes? / Juan-David Nasio ; translated by David Pettigrew.
Other titles: Inconscient, c'est la répétition English
Description: Albany, NY : State University of New York Press, [2019] |
  Series: SUNY series in Contemporary French Thought | Includes
  bibliographical references and index.
Identifiers: LCCN 2018036275 | ISBN 9781438475097 (hardcover : alk. paper) |
  ISBN 9781438475103 (pbk. : alk. paper) | ISBN 9781438475110 (ebook)
Subjects: LCSH: Psychoanalysis. | Repetition (Philosophy) | Lacan, Jacques,
  1901–1981.
Classification: LCC BF173 .N34513 2019 | DDC 150.19/5—dc23
LC record available at https://lccn.loc.gov/2018036275

10 9 8 7 6 5 4 3 2 1

Contents

2.

Translator's Acknowledgments

I would like to thank Andrew Kenyon, Acquisitions Editor in Philosophy, at the State University of New York Press, for his support of this book translation from its earliest stages, and for his ongoing support of our book series at SUNY Press devoted to Contemporary French Thought. I was grateful to be able to consult with Dr. Nasio throughout the translation process concerning crucial concepts and terms, and thank him, as always, for his infinite generosity of time and spirit. Thanks as well to my Series Co-Editor and colleague François Raffoul, for his thoughtful review of selected passages and key terms in the final preparation of the manuscript. Thanks to my friends at Hotel de Senlis, in Paris, and Hotel Saraj, in Sarajevo, where much of the work of translation took place. I was grateful to receive a Connecticut State University Research Grant, an SCSU Faculty Creative Activity Research Grant, as well as Research Time from the Office of the Dean of Arts and Sciences at Southern Connecticut State University, support that was crucial for the completion of the translation. Thanks, to our Philosophy Department Administrative Assistant Sheila Magnotti for her kind assistance throughout the process. Finally, thanks to my son Ian, for his support, and for our many conversations over the years about Dr. Nasio's work.

Preface to the English Language Edition
A Conversation with Dr. Nasio

David Pettigrew:

Dr. Nasio, in this book you state that when we love, we are always attracted by "the feature that is common to all objects loved and lost in the course of our lives" (18). You give the astonishing example of a letter that Descartes wrote to Chanut in June 1647, in which he wrote, ". . . when we are inclined to love someone without knowing the reason, we may believe that this is because of a similarity to something in an earlier object of our love, though we may not be able to identify it."[1] You also refer to Spinoza when he writes: "*Everything, insofar as it is in itself, endeavors to persist in its own being.*"[2] In response to Spinoza's statement you invoke the famous Cartesian cogito, while modifying it: "*I repeat, therefore I am*" (15). These philosophical references lead me to ask you about the extent to which philosophy has enriched your psychoanalytic thinking.

---

1. "Descartes to Chanut, 6 June 1647," in *Descartes: Philosophical Letters*, trans. and ed., Anthony Kenny (Minneapolis: University of Minnesota Press, 1970), pp. 224–25. Translation slightly modified.

2. *The Chief Works of Benedict de Spinoza*, V. II, *The Ethics*, Part III, PROP. VI, trans. R. H. M. Elwes (New York: Dover Publications, 1951), 136.

Dr. Nasio:

For me, philosophy is a discourse that concerns the inner life of the human being. Everything we know today about psychical life has already been set forth, since antiquity, by the great philosophers of the tradition. If we consider Spinoza, for example, when he speaks of "self approval"[3] [*contentement de soi*], we are struck by the realization that he had already stated, in 1660, the same idea that we are using today in our current work with our patients concerning the goal of a psychoanalytic cure. What is the goal of a psychoanalytic cure? If Spinoza could respond to this question, he would assert that the goal of psychoanalysis is "self-approval." Similarly, I would say today that the goal of an analytic cure is to *bring the patient to be happy with him- or herself, to teach him or her to better love him- or herself, and to accept him- or herself with both qualities and failings.*

David Pettigrew:

In addition to your interest in philosophy, you make beautiful reference to poetry, particularly to the famous poem by Paul Verlaine, "*Mon rêve familier*" ["My Familiar Dream"]. Indisputably, these verses punctuate the force of repetition. I wanted to ask you then about the relation between psychoanalysis and poetry, as well as literature.

Dr. Nasio:

Indeed, one might say that poets are better psychologists than psychoanalysts and philosophers, but they are people guided by feelings and not by reason. Poets are possessed of the art of depicting the essence of love in a marvelous way. They have the qualities that allow them to speak to us about desire and to make us experience it when we read

---

3. *The Chief Works of Benedict de Spinoza* V. II, *The Ethics*, Part IV, PROP. LII, trans. R. H. M. Elwes (New York: Dover Publications, 1951), 222.

a poem that touches us. They have special sensitivity to perceive the hidden movements of the other's soul, and, above all, the courage to allow their own unconscious to speak. However, a poet is not a psychoanalyst because his or her poetry does not seek to cure the suffering of the one who reads it. On the contrary, for we psychoanalysts, what is essential when we speak to our patient is not the beauty of language, but its power to reawaken the emotion that lay dormant in his or her unconscious.

David Pettigrew:

In the clinical cases that you address in the book, in particular those of Rachel and Bernard, you claim that you perceive within yourself the "unconscious fantasm" that is at the origin of their depression (7). By entering into the fantasm of the patient, or, if you will, allowing the fantasm to enter into you, you access the unconscious emotion that is at the origin of the repetition of a psycho-pathological disorder. In the case of Bernard, you indicated that you perceived, within you, the same fantasmatic emotion that he had experienced as a child and had subsequently forgotten (cf. 50). To reach this conclusion, you identified yourself with an imaginary child, the child you imagined Bernard to have been. You identified yourself with an "imaginary creature," and felt what it would have felt (51). In this way, you entered into the unconscious fantasm of your patient and you translated it into simple words with which you touched the patient. How do you manage to accomplish a way of listening that is so deep and effective?

Dr. Nasio:

First, for a listening to begin, one must **be willing to enter into the silent and inner world of the patient who suffers,** to have the desire to know the patient from within, as he or she would. What does it mean to know someone from within? It is to know them as they perceive themselves: at times confident, at time vulnerable; at times overly proud, at times scorned; at times an irresistible charmer, at times unpopular. In brief, the first and most important premise that governs therapeutic listening, is the commitment of the professional, his or her authentic desire to enter into the inner world of the man, the woman, or the child who speaks to him or her. If the analyst does not have this deliberate will to enter into the intimate universe of his or her patient and say "I want to know the patient from within better than the patient knows him- or herself," or if the analyst does not have the strong desire to open him- or herself to the other, then nothing will happen. However, if the analyst is motivated by this desire, we are sure that the analysand, sensitive to this desire for commitment, will be less defensive and more receptive.

David Pettigrew:

Now, in order to conclude our brief conversation that opens the book, let's speak about the past. You write that "the present operates as a distorting lens of the past," emphasizing that "all memory is necessarily the result of the subjective reinterpretation of a former reality and never its faithful evocation" (21). You conclude that "memory is not the past, but an act of the present, a creation of the present" (21). In a related passage you state that "we are our actualized past, we are our **actualized unconscious**; an unconscious that is not behind us but in us, gathered in the here and now of the action marking what we just established" (21–22). Could you address this idea that memory is a production of the present?

Dr. Nasio:

I am convinced that the past is the unconscious, and that our past continues to act in us at each moment of our lives. At this moment, when I speak to you, it is my past that inspires my speech. All my important acts today are inevitably actualizing my past of yesterday. In a word, every creative act involves the emergence of a past that inserts itself into the present and modifies it.

David Pettigrew:

Thank you, Dr. Nasio.

1.

Once deeds are done, whether in justice or contrary to it, not even Time, the father of all, could undo their outcome.[1]

—Pindar

In this book, I would like to show you how my psychoanalytic experience has led me to the conclusion that the unconscious is repetition. Usually, we say that the unconscious manifests itself through our slips, our parapraxes, or our dreams. This is correct. But the unconscious is much more vital and intimate for us. What is the unconscious? Without denying that the unconscious is a structure organized like a language, I prefer to consider it here as a drive, as a propulsive force. The unconscious is the sovereign force that impels us to choose the woman or the man with whom we share our lives. Contrary to general opinion, the choice of our partner is less a rational decision than it is the result of an amorous relationship whose cause is unknown to us. But the unconscious is also the force that pushes us to choose the city or the house we inhabit. All these choices that we believe to be deliberate or

---

1. Pindar, *Olympian Odes, Pythian Odes*, ed. and trans. William H. Race, Loeb Classical Library 56 (Cambridge, MA: Harvard University Press, 1997) 65.

fortuitous really take place without our actually knowing why. Nevertheless, beyond this point, we have learned from clinical experience that there is another unconscious agency that is more persistent and more mysterious to which I would like to devote this book. It is the **agency that compels us to repeat.** Our life beats to the rhythm of repetition that the unconscious impels. In the end, the unconscious is the force that pushes us to **actively** reproduce, from our earliest years, the same type of amorous attachments and the same type of painful separations that inevitably mark our affective lives. Thus repetition is both healthy and unconscious: a life drive. But, the unconscious is also the force that pushes us to **compulsively** reproduce the same failures, the same traumatic moments, and the same pathological behavior. Thus repetition is pathological and unconscious: a death drive. But whether the unconscious is a life drive or a death drive, or whether it is the cause of our repetitive behavior, healthy or pathological, the only thing certain is that it is the unconscious that determines the appearance and the reappearance of the significant events that construct our existence.

*

Now what is repetition? I would like to introduce you to the concept of repetition by sharing a clinical experience with you in which you will see how repetition is present in the genesis of the suffering of the patient and also present in the mind of the practitioner when he or she wants to understand the meaning of the patient's symptoms [*manifestations*]. It is only after this clinical example that I will share my general definition of repetition and distinguish two psychoanalytic categories: healthy repetition and pathological repetition. I will especially address the latter.

*

A Clinical Experience in which the Psychoanalyst Listens to His or Her Patient While Being Mindful of the Concept of Repetition

A while ago I received in my practice, for the first time, a young lawyer named Rachel. Rachel lived alone and suffered periodically from the effect of an inconsolable affliction. She did not know what made her sad. Gradually, in the course of our meetings, she dwelled on these attacks of inexplicable crying, her inability to stop, and on her fear that it would become a permanent problem. While Rachel spoke to me, I thought of two things. Here I must emphasize that when an analyst listens to a patient, it is imperative that he or she have two things in mind. I do not agree that the analyst must listen to his or her patients without any preconceptions. No! It is preferable that, during the session, the therapist maintain a twofold mental state: while listening to what the patient is saying, he or she has questions, hypotheses, and suppositions in mind, that is to say, a useful set of preconceptions resulting from formation and practice that are "fecund." Everything that emanates from the patient, whether verbal or non-verbal, passes through the filter of the practitioner's theoretical knowledge and previous experience, a screening that is necessary for the preliminary analysis of the general features of the clinical issues of the patient. Thus, while listening to Rachel, I had two ideas in mind relative to repetition. First, to identify the moment and the context in which the first crisis appeared in adulthood, and even better, the **very first manifestation** of sadness in her childhood. There is always a first time when the symptom appears, and this initial appearance is decisive for an understanding of the cause of the suffering. The first moments are so important because it is then that impact of a symptom has the deepest effect that cannot be erased. It is as if the first disclosure of the symptom is more revelatory of the cause than its subsequent appearances. Now, the search for this first appearance of trouble is often neglected by the practitioner, although this information is indispensable for his or her understanding of the cause of the illness. For example, we will never understand an adult neurosis if we do not identify the childhood neurosis of which it is the repetition. Any adult neurosis repeats a childhood neurosis. It should be standard practice for the practitioner, during preliminary sessions, to search for the first appearance of the problem. This is the only way that the practitioner could identify the repetitive effect that follows from the first occurrence of the problem up to the most recent. Having successfully reconstituted the chain of successive symptomatic appearances, he or she could then interpret the cause of the problem. In this sense, we recall one of the major principles of psychoanalysis: **the disturbance which seems inexplicable in the mind of the patient is always found in his or her actions;** and inversely, **the disturbance whose meaning has been interpreted does not return.** But what does it mean to say that the therapist interprets a disturbance? The significance of a disturbance is nothing other than a response to a question: Why has this disturbance been necessary? What has been the development of psychical events that made it necessary? Of what problem is it the solution? I should add: the *worst* solution. If the psychoanalyst succeeds in answering these questions, he or she will already have taken an important step in determining the cause of the illness and, moreover, a step toward curing the patient.

That being the case, let us continue. My first idea then, in Rachel's presence, was to identify when her sadness appeared for the first time, and when it reappeared subsequently. If I establish this repetitive pattern of the symptom, I can gain a glimpse of the interpretation of the symptom, determine the origin of the problem, consider a clinical diagnosis, and finally decide on a direction for the cure. With respect to the importance that I accord to the symptom, let me add that I can work with the patient for months, with little interest in the family history, but I know the history of the symptom very well. The truth of a subject, that is, what intimately defines him or her, is more his or her symptom than the family history. There is more of the unconscious in a symptom than in the memory of an important family event. What does this mean? It means that the symptom is the truth of the subject, the involuntary manifestation that individualizes and signifies it most profoundly.

But let us return to Rachel. The other idea that animates my listening is of knowing the details, **all of the details** of the onset of sadness: "On what occasion? At what time of the day? At work or in the house? And if it is in the house, in what room? Alone, with someone else present, or when thinking of someone? What physical position are you in when you feel sadness?" The knowledge of these and many other apparently insignificant details will allow me, as Freud said, to observe the unconscious of my patient. I am convinced that, in the end, these details will reveal Rachel's unconscious to me. In what way? The knowledge of these details of the scene of the symptom allows me to project myself mentally, by way of imagination, into Rachel's inner world when she feels invaded by sadness. It is very important that I clarify what "project myself mentally" means. The knowledge of the details of the scene of the symptom is not so much to inform me as it is to attune me to the way my patient experiences her suffering emotionally and physically. In this way, immersed in the scene of the symptom, I can put myself in her place, feel what she feels, and think what she thinks. However, I would like to go further. I would like to identify myself not only with the real and actual person of Rachel when she is sad, but further, to identify, if possible, with an other Rachel, a virtual, imaginary, fantasmatic Rachel, a Rachel who is a little girl or even a baby, recreated in my analytic consciousness as an abandoned and distraught child. In other words, I try first to feel what Rachel feels **consciously**, and if that is possible—whether in the preliminary sessions or later during the cure—to feel as well the supposed emotion that the little fantasmatic Rachel whom I represent to myself would feel, and of which the adult Rachel has no consciousness. Let us formulate this in another way. Our adult Rachel has felt, as a child, an emotion that is **unconscious** today, an emotion that I, the analyst, would like to experience.

Twofold Empathy:
The Exclusive Skill of the Psychoanalyst

> By feeling what the patient feels when he or she suffers, the psychoanalyst shares in the emotion, first in conscious emotion, and then in unconscious emotion.
>
> —J.-D. Nasio

By focusing on these details of the symptom—my second idea—I identify with the adult Rachel who is stricken with sadness, and on that basis, I identify with a hypothetical Rachel as a child or a baby, a victim of a traumatic abandonment. I say "hypothetical" because I do not know what little Rachel has actually experienced. No one knows, not even our current Rachel, who carries the silent pain of her abandonment within the depths of her being. I have only imagined a little distraught Rachel, and I have tried to feel what this imaginary being would have felt.

This attempt to feel, within me, the patient's conscious experience when she is plagued by her symptom—**a first empathy**—, and then her unconscious experience—**a second empathy**—implies, I would say, a significant change in level. From the ground floor at the level of the symptom, I descend to the basement at the level of the unconscious where the theatrical scene that I call the unconscious fantasm is played out. It is as if I descend from the scene of the symptom where adult Rachel knows what she is experiencing, to the scene of the unconscious fantasm where little Rachel experiences an emotion of which adult

Rachel is unaware. On the basis of my perception of Rachel's sadness when she suffers from her symptom, I pass to the perception of the emotion of which Rachel is not conscious and which, nevertheless, dominates her fantasm. It is a fantasm, I insist, that the patient does not represent to itself, and which is dominated by an emotion that the patient does not recognize.

We will return later to the notion of the unconscious fantasm. For the moment I would say that the fantasm is a diffuse scene, with faded, somewhat blurry contours, which is imprinted in the unconscious of the child at the moment of the trauma; this scene is unquestionably the hidden cause of the symptom. Behind a symptom there is always a fantasm hiding. Provisionally, a fantasm is defined as: **an unconscious memory, the trace left in the unconscious by a psychoanalytic trauma during childhood**. But the fantasm is not a passive memory, it is an open wound that does not heal and that deepens for years—from childhood until adulthood—like an infected site that contaminates the entire person. Also, I take the fantasm to be the unconscious cause of Rachel's current depression. Now it is precisely this fantasm that appears in my mind. I would like to be clear: I perceive in me, the analyst, the unconscious fantasm of my patient.

When we speak of the conscious symptom and of the unconscious fantasm, where do we situate repetition? Repetition is found at the level of emotion. The emotion experienced consciously by the patient when she suffers her symptom, **repeats** the dominant emotion of the fantasm, of which the patient is not conscious. **The current emotion repeats an unconscious childhood emotion**. In the case of Rachel, the unconscious childhood emotion appeared clearly to me when, in the course of preliminary meetings, the analysand confided in me that, having been born prematurely, she had to be placed in an incubator for a long time, and her mother, who was sick and bedridden, was unable to see her, touch her, and hold her in her arms. While thinking of this wrenching separation, I understood that the inexplicable sadness of the woman today was, in fact, the pathological repetition of the distress of the baby of the past. Thus this archaic distress caused by abandonment, which is not felt consciously by Rachel today, nor any longer by baby Rachel—because it was too violent to be registered in her immature consciousness—is precisely the unconscious primordial distress that I, the analyst, have attempted to experience. Thus, I succeeded in explaining today's pain as the return of yesterday's wound and proposed an interpretation of the symptom to the patient while seeking to cure it.

I would like to make a brief comment to close this discussion of the mental work of the psychoanalyst, and to show how the effectuation of the two empathies distinguishes psychoanalysis from other psychotherapeutic techniques. Psychoanalysis is not defined by the existence of a couch on which the patient lies or by a chair where the one who listens is located. Nor is it defined by the arrangement of furniture, or even by the original assertion of the fundamental rule of free association. Psychoanalysis is defined by the intensity of the unconscious relation between the therapist and the analysand. Such a relation depends precisely on the ability of the therapist to perceive, in his or her unconscious, the unconscious fantasm of the patient, and to enact a twofold empathy: a more superficial empathy with the conscious patient, and another more profound empathy with the unconscious patient. Certainly this perceptual experience of the psychoanalyst does not occur at every moment, or with all patients, or in all sessions. No, these are singular moments that are relatively rare and, above all, **therapeutic** because if this perceptual experience occurs and reproduces itself, that condition of the patient can be improved.

In summary, the first idea that guided my listening to Rachel[2] is a **clinical** idea: it concerns the repetition of the symptom in time,

---

2. Today, after three years of treatment, Rachel has completed her analysis. Her symptoms are significantly attenuated after having addressed with her, her sense of abandonment as an infant and having led her to relive in our sessions, as well as on numerous occasions, the cruel solitude of a premature newborn.

the number of times it was manifested since its first appearance, the number of episodes Rachel has suffered. This is what I call the **temporal repetition of the symptom**. My second idea concerning the research of the details of the scene of the symptom through which I identify with the conscious and then the unconscious emotion of the patient, is a **metapsychological** idea. It entails the **spatial or topological repetition of the fantasm**: the conscious emotion of the symptom repeats the unconscious emotion of the fantasm; Rachel's sadness as an adult repeats Rachel's distress as a baby. In addition, spatial repetition functions within psychical space: an element belonging to conscious space—the symptom—repeats an element belonging to unconscious space: the fantasm. We have thus on the one hand, the **temporal repetition of the symptom** that we can identify as **horizontal** repetition because the successive occurrences extend on the time line insofar as time is conceived of as a succession. On the other hand, we can identify the **spatial or topological repetition of the fantasm** as **vertical** repetition because the two events are superimposed, one the deeply entrenched fantasm and the other the surface symptom. The conscious symptom repeats the unconscious fantasm in a perpendicular manner. Later, we will return to the **temporal and spatial repetitions** by illustrating them with two schemas [figure 1 and figure 2 (35)].

In terms of repetition, the position of the psychoanalyst is twofold. On the one hand, he or she regards the past in order to find the milestones of a history, a history of trouble that affects the patient. On the other hand, he or she looks ahead to find the signs that emanate from the person who speaks, in order to recreate, in the theatre of the imagination, the scene of the symptom, and, if possible, the scene of the fantasm. In one case, the psychoanalyst is a **clinician** who takes note and counts; in the other case, he or she is a **metapsychologist** who supposes, deduces, intuits, and feels.

*

A General Definition of Repetition

Often I have this dream—a strange searching dream—
Of a woman I don't know, whom I love, and who loves me,
And who is not, each time, different, exactly,
But loving me, understanding me, is neither the same.

—*Paul Verlaine*[3]

But let us leave the psychoanalyst's office for the moment and consider repetition in a quite general sense of the term. What is repetition? Repetition designates a universal movement, a rhythm that rules the biological, psychical, social, and even cosmic order. For thousands of years the earth invariably repeats the same elliptical orbit around the sun. Similarly, the history of humanity constantly repeats the same conflicts and the same precarious solutions. Closer to our own experience, our body repeats indefatigably, from birth to death, the same vital gestures: respiration, consumption, elimination, sleep, etc. Our body repeats, and thanks to the repetition it consolidates itself as a body. Also, our psyche experiences the same feelings, the same thoughts and the same actions throughout life, which I am going to describe in detail. But allow me first to advance a general definition of repetition. I propose the following formulation: repetition involves at least two occurrences in which an object **appears**—a first occurrence—, disappears, and then **reappears**—a second occurrence—each

---

3. Paul Verlaine, "My Familiar Dream"/"*Mon rêve familier,*" *Poems Under Saturn,* trans. Karl Kirchwey (Princeton, NJ: Princeton University Press, 2011), 26–27.
"*Je fais souvent ce rêve étrange et pénétrant*
D'une femme inconnue, et que j'aime, et qui m'aime,
Et qui n'est, chaque fois, ni tout à fait la même
Ni tout à fait une autre, et m'aime et me comprend."

time slightly different but always recognized as the same object. Certainly, repetition is the repetition of the Same, of the same thing that reappears, but—take note!—never identical to itself, always slightly modified each time it resurges. Each time the earth revolves around the sun, an infinitesimal change occurs. The earth is each time always the same but never absolutely identical since the passage of time prevents it from remaining intact. This is very important. When I began to work on the theme of repetition, I did not understand the expression "repetition of the same." I worked on the concept for ten years and, nevertheless, each time I learned something new. For example, the sentence "Repetition is the repetition of the same object that never appears identical to itself although it is always recognizable as the same object." To write this simple sentence has taken me years! Why? Because I did not understand that repetition was always repetition of a thing that was *never* really **identical** to itself.

This is the first of three laws that determine any repetitive process: **The law of the Same and of the Different.** The Same is never repeated as identical to itself; it will always be recognizable but in different ways. In a word, repetition is the trajectory of an object identified by an observer who sees it appear, disappear, and reappear, each time slightly different, in variable moments and contexts.

However, to affirm that a thing is repeated in time, it does not suffice to state that it remains the same while undergoing modifications. It remains to be established that it absents itself between two presences. This finding justifies the second law, the law of the **alternation of Presence and Absence.**

Let us add now the third law that is essential to the movement of repetition: **The intervention of an observer who counts the number of the moments it is repeated.** This is an obvious fact that one often forgets: Without the observer there is no repetition. Why? This is because repetition is, in reality, the result of a reflective process.

There is no repetition without you, without your counting, without the conscious enumerator that you are. In order for there to be repetition there must be a human agent; there must be a consciousness that identifies an event, extracts it from the incessant flux of life, and counts all the times where it surfaces. In other words, our thinking **isolates** a prominent fact, **names** it and **counts the number of times** it is repeated. It is thus that we transform a simple fact into a **signifier**, a term central to Lacan's corpus. What is a signifier? A signifier is any event, any being or any thing that I formulate into an entity **than can be counted**. Although correct, my definition remains quite general. Psychoanalytically speaking, I should write: "A signifier is any involuntary manifestation of the subject, susceptible to being counted by the subject itself or by an other." When, for example, I enumerate Rachel's successive crises, **I transform the crises into signifiers**. Each crisis represents Rachel's unconscious in the midst of past crises and those to come. As Lacan expressed it: "A signifier represents the subject for another signifier," and paraphrasing this I would say: a crisis represents Rachel's unconscious for other past and future crises. It would be necessary here to reconsider many other aspects of Lacan's notion of the signifier, but the most important point for our position is to recall how the signifier enacts a chain in a repetitive series of similar signifiers. What is proper to a signifier is to be among other signifiers that resemble it. There is no isolated signifier, and further, there is no signifier without repetition.

A brief word regarding the human agent who counts the occurrences of repetition. If it is true that there is only repetition because a lucid agent enumerates the successive appearances, the one who counts is unaware of the repetition that traverses him or her. What does this mean? It means that we have two positions in relation to repetition: either we are external to the repetitive series that we count—in this case we remain conscious—or we are the innocent plaything of an imperceptible repetition of the same happy or unhappy event—in which case we are unconscious[4]—either we count and we remain outside of that which we count, or we are blind and involved in the irresistible flux of repetition. However, Lacan goes even further. He is not content to establish that a subject can be traversed by a repetition of which it is unaware, but insists that the subject is constituted by it. That is to say that its desire, its life, and its destiny are influenced by repetition. Here is an eloquent passage from *Écrits* where Lacan, identifying repetition with the symbolic order, proposes that the human being is the product: "Since this repetition is symbolic repetition, it turns out that the symbolic order can no longer be conceived as constituted by the human being but must rather be conceived as constituting him or her."[5]

*

The Beneficial Effects of Healthy Repetition:
Self-Preservation, Self-Fulfillment, and Identity Formation

Can we assign a goal to repetition? Does it have a goal set in advance? It is a philosopher who allows us to respond clearly to this question. In his remarkable *Ethics III*, Spinoza tries to describe all life in terms of a single fundamental tendency, the tendency of every person to "persist in his or her own being." I am always amazed by this powerful

---

4. It is a situation where we are the actor but also the spectator of a repetition that carries us. This is the case of a **revivification**. Later, when we conclude our book by evoking the phenomenon of therapeutic **revivification**, the sublime figure of repetition, we will see that at the moment of the reactivation of the traumatic emotion, the analyst is simultaneously **the one who relives the trauma** and **the one who sees the trauma revived**.

5. Jacques Lacan, *Seminar on "The Purloined Letter," Écrits*, trans. Bruce Fink (New York: W. W. Norton & Co., 2006), 34. Hereafter cited as *Écrits*, followed by the page number. Translation modified.

sentence that, in a few words, describes life. Thousands of philosophers and men of science have tried to define life. Some have declared, for example, that it is "the ensemble of functions that resist death." Others have written that it is "what one can abolish," and others write that it is "what consumes and produces waste." In the end, all these definitions emphasize the perishable nature of life. For his part, Spinoza adopted an opposite position. He revealed above all the expansive force of life, the *elan* that maintains itself without fail and triumphs over all obstacles. According to Spinoza, "Everything, insofar as it is in itself, endeavours to persist in its own being."[6] Every person, only by existing, tends to continue to exist, and attempts, in every possible way, to persist in his or her being. By writing this book, what am I doing other than persisting in my being? Our existence is a plebiscite, at every moment, on our desire to live. Each day by getting up and by doing what we have to do, we implicitly say yes to life. Now, I do not know until what point I will renew my daily reaffirmation of life. It is my body that will decide and, in addition to it, my unconscious. For the moment, faced with these two masters—my body and my unconscious—I try to limit myself to persisting in my being. I write these pages today, and will write others tomorrow, as long as my masters allow, I will persist in my being, I will follow my path.

But what does it mean to **persist** in one's being, if not to repeat and to repeat in order to conserve one's unity as an individual, to fulfill oneself—that is to say to exist to the fullest possible extent—and to reinforce one's identity in the passage of time? I repeat myself, and by repeating myself, I conserve my past because by rediscovering it each time I appropriate it; I improve myself because with each repetition, learning from experience, I gain knowledge, I learn to contextualize experience, and, in the end I consolidate my identity. Since I am forced

---

6. *The Chief Works of Benedict de Spinoza*, V. II, *The Ethics*, Part III, PROP. VI, trans. R. H. M. Elwes (New York: Dover Publications, 1951), 136.

to repeat, I confirm that I am the same today and tomorrow. In sum, *I repeat, therefore I am*. What then is the purpose of repetition? In fact, repetition does not have an external goal that it seeks to attain. It is essentially an irreducible tendency that has no other purpose than to remain a force that leads us to better ourselves. Repetition produces three primary effects: to preserve our individual unity, to develop our maximum potential, and to consolidate the feeling that we are the same yesterday and today. In addition, repetition produces a threefold beneficial effect: **self-preservation, self-fulfillment, and the affirmation of our identity.** Repetition structures us, reassures us, and enhances our well-being. While writing this last sentence, I imagined an objection raised by a reader who would say: "Routine horrifies me and I only aspire to one thing: to change, to be able to change! I adore novelty while repetition wearies me." I would respond: "Certainly we all love surprises, the freshness of the new, novel feelings, and births of every kind. Nothing is more beautiful! We love being astonished and even disconcerted." How many times has it happened when I address a patient and say: "At this moment you need to be surprised as boredom is weighing you down!" It is indisputable that the idea of the new excites us, and nevertheless I ask you to reflect a moment on the choice between the pleasure of the new and the comfort of the familiar. Obviously this is a choice that we will never face because the old is always dissimulated in the guise of the new. Nothing can be entirely new or entirely not-new. In fact, the new does not exist in a pure form. I challenge you to find something new that is completely deprived of a trace of the past. And then, between the old and the new, it is the old that wins. What does this mean? We change and grow old, while in our hearts we feel constantly the same whatever age we happen to be. This sameness [*mêmeté*] in us is the timeless heart of our being. So the old triumphs over the alterations of time. I am essentially the same at 6 months, 2 years, at 40 and 60 years, in spite of the innumerable changes that modified me. I change but I remain always the same. This certitude of the sameness [*mêmeté*] reassures me and enhances my well-being.

I wrote earlier, *I repeat, therefore I am.* Now I must modify the formulation as follows: "*I am what I repeat.*" This is not a trivial play on words but a way of completing our understanding of the role of repetition in the affirmation of our identity. I proposed that by repeating myself I consolidated my intimate feeling of being myself. Now, I would like to show you that my identity is not only a feeling but also an entity external to me: a person, a thing, or an abstract idea. My identity is within me and outside of me. I will explain. If I were a woman I would say: "The man that I love today strangely resembles the man I loved twenty years ago and each of the men have something that reminds me of my mother when I was six years old." I just wrote "mother" and not "father" as one would have expected. Experience teaches me that in the amorous choice that a woman makes concerning a man, the mother is much more determining than the father. It is contrary to our opinion that the woman's choice operates on the basis of the Oedipal love for the father. I insist that this is often false! In the selection of her masculine partner, the woman is compelled to repeat the pre-Oedipal love for the mother rather than the Oedipal love for her father. When she chooses a man, we generally find the mother as the profound cause of the choice, and the father as more superficial. The woman chooses her companion under the influence, above all, of the unreasoned, unconscious relation with her mother and then under the influence of the more superficial relation of seduction with the father. This is why the partner can reinvest this or that aspect, psychically reproducing those of the father, but the essential affective attachment that links the woman to the man reproduces the unconscious attachment to the mother. And even in the case where the woman chose her partner based on the model of her father or her brother, when carried away by anger during a domestic scene, she would transfer the hateful feelings that she harbored for her mother during the Oedipal age or during adolescence onto her husband. This is a proposition that I submit for the readers. Think of a man who shares your life and ask yourself if—viscerally, and more profoundly than your love or deceptions—the relation that unites you to him is not paradoxically marked by the most carnal love and by the most bitter reproaches that linked you libidinally to your mother. In sum, one repeats with one's partner, the passionate and conflictual bond with one's mother from childhood or adolescence. I specify immediately that when I use the term "mother" I am not referring to the real person who was your mother, but the idea of the mother that you forge within yourself. If you consider, for example, the case of twin sisters, they each develop a completely different vision of their mother. Inevitably, each of us forges an idea of the mother or of the father that is different from what they really are. It is the projection of this invented image on the man that will finally decide the choice of the partner. When I wrote at the beginning of the book that the unconscious is a force that impels us to choose the man or the woman with whom to share our lives, I was thinking precisely of the powerful influence of the fantasm that we project on the other during the crucial decisions of our existence.

My identity is thus to be understood in two distinct and complimentary ways. First, it is the feeling of being myself consolidated with each repetition. But my identity is also external to me, in the man or the woman with whom I live. It is in him or her that my identity, and consequently, in him or her where my unconscious, is incarnated. **My unconscious is also outside me, in the other on which I depend affectively**. Here, I must make an important remark with respect to identity outside the self. I just wrote that my identity is found in the man or the woman with whom I share my life, but it is necessary to go further and explain that my identity is not in the person of my actual partner, but in a feature that characterizes him or her. Now, this feature that distinguishes the man or the woman whom I love, has been also shared by every person I have loved since my birth. We love without realizing that our loved one today has a feature in common with one whom we loved yesterday and that our successive partners, beginning with our father or our mother, have also had this common feature. Effectively, when one meets someone new, one is often surprised to find that he or she bears a characteristic of the person who was previously loved and desired. This feature, a special smile, for example, which persists and is repeated in the first, second, and all of the successive partners in one's history; this feature, this smile, is a feature and this feature is at the core of who we ourselves are. Yes, we are the feature that is common to all objects loved and lost in the course of our lives. Also, **I love you not for what you are but for that part of me that you carry within you.** Who then am I? I am the smile that lights up your face. My identity is not reducible to a feeling of being myself, it is materialized in that part of me that shines in the man or the woman with whom I share my life. It is there where my identity resides and, consequently, it is there that my unconscious is also incarnated.

In order to conclude our considerations concerning identity and repetition I cannot resist sharing an astonishing confidence from Descartes in which he confirms our thesis on the unconscious attachment to a feature: one loves a loved one not for what he or she is but because he or she is the bearer of a feature that makes him or her desirable to us. Now let us listen as our philosopher confides his secret to us:

> . . . when I was a child, I loved a little girl of my own age, who had a slight squint. The impression made by sight in my brain when I looked at her cross eyes became so closely connected to the simultaneous impression arousing in me the passion of love, that for a long time afterwards when I saw cross-eyed persons I felt a special inclination to love them simply because they had that defect. At that time I did not know that was the reason for my love; and as soon as I reflected on it and recognized that it was a defect, I was no longer affected by it. So, when we are inclined to

love someone without knowing the reason, we may believe that **this is because of a similarity to something in an earlier object of our love, though we may not be able to identify it.**[7]

When I discovered this passage, I was struck by the contemporary nature of a thought that precedes us by more than three centuries! But also, inversely, I was struck by the traditional character [*ancienneté*] of our psychoanalytic reflections today. It is as if thought deploys and repeats itself in a timeless manner. But whether it is Descartes, or a psychoanalyst in the twenty-first century who interrogates the workings of love, let us remember that the nature of amorous emotion and the selection of our partner always remains an impenetrable mystery.

I would like to end this section by referring to the two formulations that define the identity produced by repetition: "I repeat therefore I am," and "I am what I repeat." In one case, the identity is the feeling of being myself, consolidated by all the repetitions that I carry out in my life. In the other case, the identity is the sum of the persons, the things, or the ideas that, over the course of the years, perdure and affirm themselves as being part of me.

*

Three Modes of the Return of Our Past: In Our Consciousness, in Our Healthy Actions and in Our Pathological Actions

We just defined repetition by establishing its beneficial effects, and after dwelling at length on the identity/repetition dyad, we have concluded

---

7. "Descartes to Chanut, 6 June 1647," in *Descartes: Philosophical Letters*, trans. and ed., Anthony Kenny (Minneapolis: University of Minnesota Press, 1970), 224–25. Translation slightly modified.

with a twofold definition of identity as the intimate feeling of the self, and as the extension of the ego in the external world. Now I would like to respond to the question concerning what repeats itself in us, which is the object of repetition. Let us say immediately that what is repeated in me is what has already taken place: my past, a past that constantly returns in the present in three modes of resurgence of the past in the present—in **consciousness**, in **healthy actions**, and in **pathological actions**. In psychoanalysis, we call these latter two categories of the return of the past in actions, **repetition**. Let us add that for us, **repetition** is always **unconscious**. In effect, if the act is, obviously, consciously perceived by the subject who accomplishes it, its cause remains unknown. This is why the phrase "unconscious repetition" signifies a repetition whose cause is unconscious.

The first return of the past, the most ordinary, is the one we refer to as the conscious return of the past. This is the case of a memory that reproduces a memory from another time. The memories are most often visual images but they can also be sonorous, tactile, olfactory, or even gustatory impressions such as that of the celebrated madeleine that returns Proust to the sweet memory of his childhood. This return of the past to consciousness is thus **re-memoration**. But before approaching the other major form of the return of the past, the return of our actions or **repetition**, I would like to reflect on the quality of past that we retrieve as memory. Is our past real, the one that we have effectively experienced? Certainly not. Memory is always capricious and unfaithful. The past that returns to consciousness is only the distant reflection of a reality never lost, a reality that we inevitably capture as distorted by the prism of our current perception. This is why the memory of our past is only the distorted product of an illusory reconstruction. When we think for example of the house of our childhood, invariably we imagine it being large, but if we return to it, we are disappointed to find that it is so small. The house that the little boy left is no longer the same in the eyes of the mature man he has become. Thus, the present operates as a distorting lens of the past. Henceforth, all memory is necessarily the result of the subjective reinterpretation of a former reality and never its faithful evocation. It is only the past remodeled and recreated in the light of our present perception. This is why we will say that the memory is not the past but an act of the present, a creation of the present.

Now we will approach the second major mode of the resurgence of the past that I refer to as **repetition**. **It is no longer as a memory that the past returns, but in the form of an experience, of a comportment, or of a crucial choice that the subject makes without knowing it is its own past that, by being repeated, causes him or her to make such a decision or accomplish such an action**. My past is thus no longer evoked by a conscious memory, but precipitated in the essential actions of my life, actions that at the time I consider deliberate or fortuitous, but that in truth are the repetition of a past seeking to reappear. Yes, our essential actions, such as the one, for example, of choosing our partner, the work that we do, or even the place where we live, are all decisive choices that, without our knowledge, actualize the past. Now each return of the past in our actions, each important moment of our lives, is an addition, a new layer that is added, and that rests on the former layers that constitute the basis of our personality. What are we, in fact, what is our ego today, if not the sedimentation of all of the returns in our actions of a past that is affectively intense and often troubled? As a whole, no doubt, our past follows us at every instant: what we felt, thought, or wanted since our first awakening, and even before, is there, acting in the present. **We are our past in action**. Yes, the person that we are, in this fleeting moment, is the latest repetition of our past. While addressing you, the reader, I am in this moment the outcome of all that I have been, of all the happy or difficult experiences that I have endured. And I would say, as in the well-known song—*"Non, je ne regrette rien!"* [No, I regret nothing!]—since all that preceded me has led me to be the one that I am today, for you, and for myself. In brief, we are our actualized past, we are our **actualized unconscious**; an unconscious that is not behind us but in us, gathered in the here and now of the action marking what we just established. When Edith Piaf sang: *"Non, rien de rien, non, je ne regrette rien,"* this was not a neurotic who lamented and who would like to relive her past. On the contrary, it was a subject proud of its past, even if it was stormy at times, a subject at peace with itself, and at peace with its own unconscious. While the satisfied subject accepts, indeed loves the unconscious that makes it be what it is, the neurotic in crisis, tormented by its history, struggles with itself, against its own unconscious that horrifies it because the decisions that it makes or the actions that it takes result in the same failures or errors.

We have thus **the return, in a healthy action**, of an affectively intense past that is troubled and **repressed**; and the **return, in a pathological action**, of a not simply troubled, but a **traumatic past**. I will conclude by saying that the traumatic past is **foreclosed and repressed**. I explain the term "foreclosed" in the following chapter. For the moment let us say that the first form of repetition in action is that of an unconscious that we assimilate to the life drives that seek to sustain existence. The other form of repetition in action is the return of a traumatic past. It is the violent actualization of an unconscious that we assimilate to the death drives that, in contrast to the life drives, reduce the person to a traumatic core. The life drives bond, integrate, and sustain the person, while the death drives separate, isolate, and reduce the person to its most tense and painful state. When it is the unconscious life force that rises to the surface of the ego, the past inserts itself quite naturally into the present action, joins forces with life, and is often manifest through creative acts. When, on the contrary, it is the unconscious force of death that is precipitated in wild and compulsive action, the past undermines and destabilizes us. In the case of the unconscious force of life, it is a question of a troubled past, and therefore **repressed**, while waiting to return to integrate itself into the present when the circumstances of the moment require it. In the case of the unconscious force of death, what is at issue is a traumatic past that is therefore **foreclosed** before being **repressed**. It is a past that impatiently seeks to externalize itself repetitively by brutally piercing the shell of the ego and taking the form of a symptom, or of acting out. I am anticipating my presentation of the next chapter by telling you that the trauma—a synonym for traumatic emotion—once experienced, foreclosed, and repressed, is an impatience to be relived, again and again. Trauma is paradoxically a drug, and the one who is tramautized is addicted to this drug. **Trauma engenders trauma.**

The three returns of our past can be delineated in the following way.

The three returns of our past:

➤ **Re-memoration** is the return to consciousness of a **forgotten** past.

➤ **Healthy** | repetition | is the return, in our behavior, of a **troubled** and **repressed** past.

➤ **Pathological** | repetition | is the compulsive return, in our **symptoms** and in our **acting out**, of a **traumatic, foreclosed**, and **repressed** past.

It is precisely the pathological and compulsive repetition that leads many patients to seek analysis, which we will address now.

Pathological Repetition is the Compulsive Return of a Traumatic Past that Erupts in the Present as a Symptom or as an Impulsive Action

"The unconscious *impulses do not want to be remembered* . . . but endeavour *to reproduce themselves* . . . the patient seeks to put his or her passions *into action*"[8]

—Sigmund Freud

---

8. "The Dynamics of Transference," Sigmund Freud, *The Standard Edition of the Complete Psychological Works of Sigmund Freud*, Vol. XII., trans. James Strachey (London: The Hogarth Press, 1986), 108. Hereafter cited as SE followed by the Volume and page number.

What then is pathological repetition? I respond straightaway by modifying the general definition that I suggested earlier: **pathological repetition involves** *at least three occurrences*—and not two, because it is insistent and compulsive—**in which a violent and repressed childhood emotion appears, disappears, reappears, and reappears once again, years later in adulthood, in the form of a troubling experience for which the symptom and acting out are paradigms**. But what is the traumatic past that always returns in a similar way? What is the nature of the childhood emotion that precipitates in the present and causes suffering? Let us say clearly: the "return" of pathological repetition, the Same [*le Même*] that haunts the subject, is a blind and violent emotion experienced in childhood or puberty, during a half-real, half-imagined traumatic episode of a sexual, aggressive, or sad character, in which the subject is at the center of the event, whether as victim, actor, or witness. Such an emotion that strikes the child or young adolescent before it is repressed, is not a pure emotion. One cannot say, in a perfunctory way that "the child has been sexually abused," or that "the child has been mistreated," or even that "the child has been abandoned." No. All those formulations are appropriate but do not express what the child has actually experienced, the impact that it encountered at the time. The terrible childhood emotion is in fact composed of extreme and contradictory emotions, a mixture of fright, disgust, and sometimes pleasure: all experienced by a child who is **sexually abused**.[9] It is a mixture of fear,

---

9. It is difficult to write that a child, boy or girl who suffers a sexual attack can experience pleasure, even if it is a frightening pleasure that it is inassimilable by an immature ego. Nevertheless it is a reality established by all clinicians, and in particular by Freud when he wrote: "Not all sexual experiences release unpleasure; most of them release pleasure. Thus the reproduction of most of them is linked with uninhibitable pleasure. An uninihibitable of this kind constitutes a *compulsion*." ("Letter 52, December 6, 1896," SE I, 236)

pain, hatred, and in certain cases, pleasure—all quite extreme—experienced by the child who is **mistreated**. Finally, it is a mixture of fear, sadness, and even hatred, experienced by a child who is **abandoned**. I designate these mixtures of exacerbated emotions with the Lacanian term "jouissance." What is jouissance? In the context of our treatment of repetition, I would define it in the following way: *Jouissance is the concretion of blind, violent, and contradictory emotions experienced by the traumatized child. Such emotions are experienced but not registered by a consciousness that is immature and overwhelmed by the impact. Jouissance is then a mixture of emotions that are experienced but not consciously represented, felt in a confused way and not unassimilated by the traumatized ego.* "*I cannot say*"—declared an analysand remembering a sexual assault—"*that I experienced the feelings and emotions then. I understood nothing, I was paralyzed, trembling, throbbing.*" This strange phenomenon of experiencing an overflowing emotion, without being consciously aware of the experience, and *without being able to represent it symbolically*, I identify as the **foreclosive** blow [*l'ictus forclosif*]. In fact, the child, shaken by the trauma, forecloses the jouissance: the child feels it in its body but does not represent it mentally. It is as if it is struck by **emotional agnosia**, that is to say that it does not recognize the emotions and the sensations that it perceives. It perceives them without representing them mentally. It is the exclusion of jouissance from the world of representations, from the symbolic world, which makes it more virulent and more determined than ever to resurge as such, identical to itself. Also, as a blind and violent emotion, rejected from the symbolic, the child's jouissance becomes an uncontrollable emotion that wants to charge the adult body with its burning tension a thousandfold. Earlier I wrote: "Trauma engenders trauma," and now I translate it as "**Jouissance engenders jouissance.**" I would like to raise anew the question of the compulsive character of jouissance and respond in a synthetic manner:

Why does an adult subject tend to repeat—
without its knowledge—an experience that was as
painful as the childhood trauma to which it was subjected,
when common sense would lead us to believe
that he or she would rather forget it?
Why does jouissance seek to resurge compulsively?

We have four possible and complementary responses: symbolic, economic, clinical, and genetic.

➤ *First, the* **symbolic** *response. The cause of the compulsive repetition of jouissance is found in three words:* **the failure of symbolization.** *Lacan* **once said "Whatever is refused in the symbolic order ... reappears in the real."**[1] *I would paraphrase this in the following way: jouissance excluded from the symbolic compulsively reappears in the real as an uncontrollable action. Yes, it is the non-symbolization of jouissance, that is, to its foreclosure, its non-representation in consciousness and its non-integration into the ego of the child that is the origin of its persistent repetition. Why? Because any strong emotion that is not anchored in consciousness by a representation, once relegated to the unconscious, remains* **isolated,** *that is to say, cut from the network of all other unconscious representations that communicate amongst themselves. It is this isolation, this segregation that closes jouissance on itself and prevents the distribution of its excess charge of tension among other representations. Jouissance is loose in the unconscious like a fireball seeking an opportunity to surface and overwhelm the body once again.* **It is originary jouissance in a young body, and it wants to revive jouissance in the adult body.**

➤ *However, we will advance another symbolic response. Since jouissance is not attached to a representation, we can suppose that the compulsive tendency to reappear is in fact a quest for the representation that it lacks. In effect, the recurrent symptom or the unpredictable behavior in which it seeks to externalize itself can be considered as a call addressed to someone who is capable of naming it and finding the representation that can calm it. Symbolization subdues jouissance because it allows it to "socialize" by integrating itself into the set of ordinary emotions.*

➤ *I will turn now to the* **economic** *response. Traumatic childhood jouissance, isolated and overcharged with tension, seeks to be re-experienced in an impulsive manifestation that operates as a valve for the release of energy. An original jouissance is repeated and is repeated as its excessive tension that is unable to be released.*

➤ *The* **clinical** *response is centered on anxiety. During the traumatic episode the sudden and massive aggression of which the child was the victim did not permit time for anxiety, or to flee the danger and defend oneself. Anxiety would have permitted the fear of and preparation for the danger, but such anxiety was lacking. Having been subjected to a childhood trauma the adult subject seeks to find, particularly in nightmares, a similarly dangerous situation and to relive the same experience, but this time while feeling anxiety. Also, the subject tries to transform the terror into anxiety.*

➤ *The final response is a* **genetic** *response. Since his first work, Freud considered that the traumatized subject remains* **fixated** *on the unhealthy experience of satisfaction that has signified its trauma. It is as if the child who was assaulted had a deficient prototype for responding to massive excitations imprinted in its unconscious. Also, the adult subject would not know any other mode of satisfaction than the brutal one experienced during the trauma. This is why we find men and women who come to analysis because they cannot stop their irrepressible quest for the same pleasure blended with pain—jouissance—that they experienced during the trauma*

> *suffered as a child. Henceforth, one can explain the cause of the pathological repetition as* **the irresistible attraction exercised by an exclusive and unhealthy model of satisfaction.**
>
> ➤ *Why does jouissance seek to compulsively return? It returns in order to be named, in order to be discharged, to be completed by anxiety and above all because its nature is to remain a jouissance. Fundamentally, whether it aspires to be named, discharged or tempered by anxiety, all these quests are only intentions that we attribute to it. In reality,* **jouissance wants nothing, and it does not want anything to change.** *It wants to obstinately continue its movement and remain identical to itself.*

At this point, I would like to reconsider the sequence of the different stages of the genesis of jouissance.

A **psychical trauma** in the child is a massive influx and experience of an excitation in a childhood ego that is too weak to resist:

- The violent eruption in the child of an emotional magma that we have named **jouissance**.

- The **foreclosure** of jouissance, or the lack [défaut] of symbolization.

- The **repression** of unbearable jouissance at the very moment of the trauma, that is to say, a rejection into the unconscious.

- Once relegated to the unconscious, jouissance remains repressed for several years.

- During this period, **repressed, isolated,** and **roaming,** jouissance is active, ferments and only aspires to one thing: to surface and implode in the adult body.

Now, the traumatized child that has been unable to forge a **symbolic representation** of what was experienced, manages nevertheless, unconsciously, to fashion jouissance into a **pictorial representation** that is more elementary than a conscious ideational representation. Lacking conscious representation, jouissance crystalized in an **unconscious representation** that Freud identified as a "representation of a thing." Repressed jouissance is then crystallized in a scene where the action gels and that I call a "**fantasmatic scene**." It is a scene that is barely sketched, with blurred contours, excessive tension, drifting in the unconscious, and eager to externalize itself. What kind of scene? It is a very imprecise painting, composed of two or three characters who are acting, or at times, a fragment, a scene, where one sees a part of the body of one of the characters embracing a part of the body of the other.

Here is a brief example drawn from the case of Bernard who you are going to meet again in the last chapter. When he was little, Bernard witnessed a violent and bloody dispute between his parents, feeling confusedly **paralyzed** in the face of what he saw: the **fear** and the **pain** of his injured mother, **rage** against his brutal father and **powerless** from being unable to intervene. This little boy could only retain, unconsciously, the fixed image of the slender neck of the mother in the grip of the father who was screaming his hatred. Let us take another example, that of a prepubescent girl, a victim of being touched, whose unconscious retains the fleeting impression of the charged scene of mixed emotions including **fear, disgust**, but also **arousal**, provoked by the rubbing of her older brother's erection on her arm. In this case, it is a predominantly tactile image, a scene that will hover in the unconscious of the child, of the adolescent, and of the adult woman that she will become. I emphasize that it "will hover in the unconscious," and not that it "will appear consciousness." In order for such a charged tactile image of disgust and pleasure to become conscious, it is necessary for the work of psychoanalysis to enact a transferential relation of trust with the patient, such that she can relive the traumatic jouissance and manage to dissipate it. Later, I will address in detail the way Bernard relived his traumatic emotion during the therapeutic process. Even if it is difficult for us to accept, the visual, auditory, tactile, or olfactory scene that anchors and dramatizes jouissance hovers [*erre*] in the unconscious without the subject managing to represent it consciously. **Throughout its life, the traumatized child will be impregnated by a parasitic toxic scene of which it is unaware, a scene that nevertheless dictates its actions and compulsive choices.**[10]

It is precisely this representational scene of jouissance, this emotional pantomime, that I refer to as the "**unconscious fantasmatic scene**,"[11] and that I take as an uncontrollable object that constantly tends to externalize itself, that is to say, to manifest itself in a symptom or in an unintended action. Earlier I said that the Same that is repeated is itself jouissance. Now I would add: yes, it is jouissance, but it is staged and encapsulated in a fantasm. So, when I say that the object that is repeated is "the Same," "jouissance," or "the unconscious fantasm," my assertions are equivalent. However, reflecting on analytic experience, the most accurate formulation would be as follows: the Same that is repeated, that constantly appears, disappears, and reappears compulsively as a psychopathological problem, is a **fantasm** loose in the unconscious. Do not confuse the traumatic past that is repeated in the present with the past that is gone, the one of happy and unhappy distant events that can be remembered or not by the subject. No. The past that interests us is the disturbed and repressed past, in the case of healthy repetition,

---

10. I would like to clarify this and say that many traumatized children have been able, over the course of their lives, to find the resource necessary to weaken the toxic scene and stop the repetition.

11. A fantasmatic scene is the trace left by a psychical trauma in the unconscious of a child or a pre-adolescent who has been the victim of a sexual assault, mistreatment or abandonment; or even has regularly suffered **micro traumas** during a period of his or her life, during the Oedipus complex, for example, when one of the parents responds to the child's erotic solicitation. I would offer the following formulation. *The fantasmatic scene is the unconscious memory of a childhood psychical trauma.*

and above all, the traumatic past in the case of pathological repetition. However, in the course of our everyday practice, we often encounter patients who, while not being gravely neurotic, nevertheless experience periods of crisis due to the eruption of a periodically traumatic past. Let us recall now that "**forgotten**" is not a synonym for "**repressed**." I can **remember** a past that is forgotten but can **enact** my repressed past (healthy repetition) or my traumatic past (pathological repetition). The latter is a past harboring an overexcited unconscious fantasm that is anxious to externalize itself, rising repetitively to the surface of the ego in the form of a compulsive manifestation.

Now we have the full story. The object of pathological repetition is an unconscious fantasm. But how does it repeat itself? It is a matter of a twofold repetition: in time and in intra-psychic space. In time, we see a recurrent symptom repeated; and in intra-psychic space, we see the same symptom repeat the unconscious fantasm of which it is the reflection on the surface of the ego (see figures 1 and 2). This is why I told you at the beginning that when an analyst is faced with a psychopathological disturbance, he or she must automatically count the number of times that the disturbance is repeated in time, and suppose that an unconscious fantasmatic scene is behind it. It is a fantasmatic scene that must first be reconstructed intellectually and then perceived intuitively, before bringing the patient to make it conscious and relive it emotionally. We will return to this in more detail with the case of Bernard.

Two Modalities of Pathological Repetition: Temporal Repetition and Topological Repetition.

Temporal repetition is a series of topological repetitions that succeed each other on a timeline.

—J.-D. Nasio

The moment has come to address the two modalities of pathological repetition in greater detail. The **temporal repetition** of the symptom is an identifiable repetition that can be counted: the patient endures it, takes account of it, and shares it. Isabelle, for example, during our first session, listed quite innocently the moments of her addiction to sex: "I had sexual relations with my older brother for a number of years between the ages of 10 and 14; then at 25, I met a man who introduced me to sadomasochistic practices, and now fifteen years hence, when I thought that I had turned the page on all that, I have reverted to the same deviant behavior. I just met a man I am madly in love with, a man who is older than I am, with whom I have sadomasochistic relations. I am afraid of losing everything, my children, my marriage, my career, and at the same time I am bewitched, I cannot do without my lover. I feel lost. I do not know what I should do." This is a glimpse of the way a patient spontaneously recounts the temporal repetition of his or her symptom. Further, I have to point out the way that Isabelle's narrative, which we just heard, eloquently illustrates the genesis of jouissance and its compulsive return. We can think that during the four years of the incestuous relation with her older brother, she was not a victim of a brutal and singular trauma, but of a series of regular micro traumas. Indeed, a psychical trauma does not necessarily present itself as a sudden and violent breach [*effraction*]. Rather, it can occur progressively and subtly over the course of a sufficiently long duration. But whether the trauma is a brutal breach or a slow and insidious succession of micro traumas, it is always defined according to an essential formulation: too much excitement in a subject who is too weak to bear it. I specify that, whether instantaneous or progressive, a psychical trauma invariably involves the failure of symbolization, a foreclosure of jouissance experienced by an immature subject (in the case of Isabelle, a pre-adolescent). Whether the failure of symbolization takes the form of a **foreclosive blow** in the case of a sudden trauma, or of what I call a **foreclosive accretion** in the case of a prolonged trauma (regular micro traumas), it always carries out a foreclosure of jouissance and its correlate, the triggering of a compulsive movement. Also, in the example of Isabelle, the older incestuous jouissance reappeared compulsively on the occasion of the two sadomasochistic adventures. Her addiction to perverse sexual practices is nothing other than her insatiable thirst to find again the same sensations and emotions of cruel pleasure awakened by her brother.

But let us return to our discussion by emphasizing that unlike temporal repetition, **spatial repetition** is not recognized by the patient but deduced by the practitioner. It is a matter of an internal, intra-psychical repetition that we identify as **topological repetition**. Topological comes from "topos," which means "place." This is the same word that Freud used to designate the two successive approaches of the psychical apparatus. The first topos was the triad of the Unconscious, Preconscious, and Conscious; and the second was the Id, the Ego, and the Superego. Simply, I call the repetition that happens between the Unconscious and Conscious: "topological." A symptom or an acting out that our patient experiences consciously, repeats the fantasmatic scene enclosed in the unconscious. I add that topological repetition can be seen as a causal repetition since the symptom from which we suffer is the effect of the toxic power of the unconscious scene. Finally, I know that while proposing the concept of topological repetition to you, I have introduced you to the abstract domain of metapsychology, but I want to show how we speculate when we are attentive to the unconscious of our patient.

In addition, topological repetition governs the essential mechanism of the symbolic: something belonging to one domain, substitutes for another belonging to another domain. What is proper to the symbol is to be a substitute. To drink a glass, for example, substitutes the act of drinking alcohol. The *glass* symbolizes alcohol. It repeats in language something—alcohol—that belongs to the real.

Now I would like to schematize these two movements of repetition with a figure. I refer you to figure 1. You can see there the two movements inherent to the operation of repetition: the trajectory of **horizontal repetition** where the recurrent symptom successively appears, disappears, and reappears; and the trajectory of a **vertical repetition** where the unconscious fantasm arises and externalizes itself compulsively in the form of a signifier or an acting out. We represent the **horizontal movement** by an axis oriented from left to right on which the different occasions where the symptom is repeated appear, as Sy^1, Sy^2 . . . Sn, that is to say, all the occasions where the unconscious fantasm externalizes itself. Correlatively, we represent the **vertical movement** by axes oriented from the bottom to the top, symbolizing the compulsive eruption of the unconscious fantasmatic scene and its symptomatic manifestation. Also, the fantasmatic scene divides itself as latent and manifest: as latent it is repressed; as manifest it takes the form of disturbance of which the patient complains. When I speak of *topological* repetition I mean that in the repressed fantasm and in the symptom that expresses it, the same jouissance, the same emotion is present, except that in the fantasm, it is unconscious and not felt, while in the symptom, it is conscious and felt. The core of jouissance that is common to the fantasm and to the symptom is noted in figure 2 with the letter @.

As you see, figure 2 completes figure 1 by showing not only that the fantasm and the symptom enclose a common jouissance @, but by also illustrating that a unique unconscious fantasm flows to the surface of consciousness in the form of balloons, Sy^1, Sy^2 . . . Sy^n that symbolize the successive occurrences of a symptom. The repeated symptom is never identical to itself. This is why I have drawn the same balloon several times but decorated with distinctive marks to indicate that it is always the same with each appearance, but affected by a slight difference.

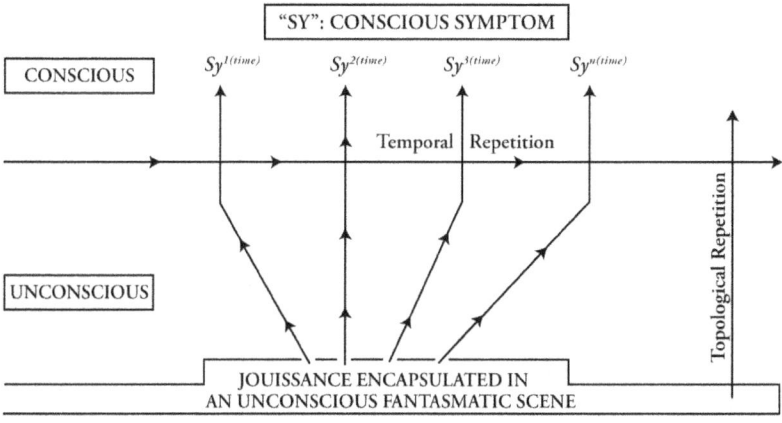

Figure 1. Two categories of pathological repetition: *temporal and topological.* ❑ In the horizontal *temporal* repetition the symptom is repeated several times on the timeline, Sy¹, Sy², . . . Syⁿ ❑ In the vertical *topological* repetition the conscious symptom, for example, Sy², repeats (externalizes) the unconscious fantasm.

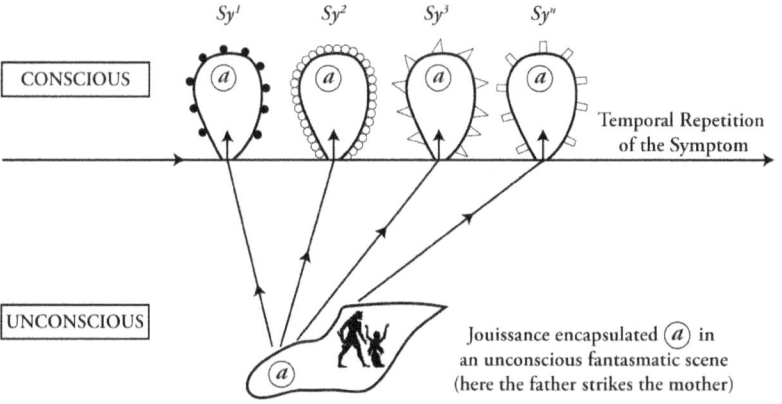

Figure 2. The balloons Sy¹ . . . Syⁿ symbolize the moment when the same symptom is repeated in a slightly different way. Each balloon is also the conscious manifestation of an unconscious fantasmatic scene. The letter ⓐ designates the unconscious jouissance encapsulated in the fantasm, and the same jouissance, this time conscious, inherent in the symptom.

I differentiate thus between two kinds of repetition: temporal repetition, which is a horizontal leap into the time that passes, and topological repetition, which is a vertical leap in intra-psychical space. But whether the first is a ricochet on a timeline, and the second a surfacing to consciousness, both are impetuous and violent, triggered by the high tension of unconscious trauma. Pathological repetition is not only painful in its manifestation, but also compulsive in its eruption. Compulsive means that it is uncontrollable and that nothing stops it. Repetition is compulsive because it results from an irresistible double force of the unconscious fantasm: a push upward in order to externalize itself, and a push forward in order to begin again. Every compulsion bears this double movement upward and forward. In other words, everything that is traumatic, that is to say, infantile, non-symbolic, foreclosed, repressed, isolated and overactive, seeks imperiously to actualize itself. Every actualization of the trauma wants to reproduce itself immediately. I will assert this more generally: **any emergence of unconscious trauma is a compulsive eruption that breaks the surface of the ego and reproduces itself in time**.

Before proceeding, I would like to summarize my perspective on pathological repetition. Repetition is the compulsive externalization of the foreclosed and repressed in the form of a disturbance that is generally painful, and is experienced by a subject, who, without knowing it, acts out his or her past instead of remembering it. When one reads the word "repetition" in Freud's text, one notes that it most often condensed three ideas: that the repeated object is an irreducible unconscious emotion—jouissance—embedded in a fantasm; that this fantasmatic jouissance tends irresistibly to manifest itself and manifests itself ceaselessly; and that, having succeeded at externalizing itself, it crystallizes itself in an imperious need to replay the traumatic experience in a recurrent symptom, in a repetitive failure, in an obsessive compulsive disturbance, in addictive behavior, in dangerous acting out, or even in sexual perversion. I gather all these manifestations under the expression **pathologies of repetition**. To repeat is always to repeat jouissance and to repeat it compulsively in a personality or behavioral disturbance. However, we have seen (on page 23) that repetition is not always the pathological repetition of a traumatic and painful past. It also exists in the active return of a healthy, albeit troubled past that is extremely exciting and emotionally intense.

*

The Drive is the Compulsive Force of Jouissance

Thus far we have responded to the following questions: What is the object that is repeated? Why is it repeated? and, How is it repeated? We have established that the **object** was jouissance, or the fantasmatic scene that depicts it. Further, we have established that the **cause** of compulsive repetition was the failure of the symbolization of said jouissance and its consequences, namely, its isolation in the unconscious and its compulsive fury; and finally, that these **two modes** of repetition were temporal and topological. Now we need to respond to a new and very important question: how can the impetuous **force** of jouissance, that very force that nourishes the unconscious fantasm and pushes it to externalize itself, be defined? The concept of the drive that is also a force must now be introduced. It is a force that leads the fantasm to rise compulsively and repetitively to the surface of the ego. Now, one can wonder how jouissance and drive can be distinguished since both are forces in action. In fact, we are dealing with the same energetic phenomenon, but considered from two different perspectives. We speak of **jouissance** when we think of emotions that oppress the traumatized child subject, of the emotions dramatized by the characters of the fantasm, and of emotions that disturb the adult subject revealing pathologies of repetition. Jouissance is the name we apply to this same psychical energy when it takes the appearance of an emotion. On the other hand, we speak of a **drive** when we think of the *trajectory* of this same psychical energy when it burns with all its passion to manifest itself; and above all when we think of the bodily *source* from which it issues forth, namely, the erogenous zones: orifices, skin, or muscles—that give birth to it. Also, the drive is what we call psychical energy when it appears as a force that emerges from the flesh. In other words, the drive is a force that arises in an excited zone of the body, rises also immediately in the mind, finds a fantasmatic scene that represents it (representation of the thing), and only aspires to discharge its tension as quickly as possible by triggering the motor action that can relieve the excitation that gave rise to it.

I will not dwell here any longer on the general definition of the drive. I prefer to concentrate now on our problem of the compulsion to repeat. I remind you that at the beginning of his work Freud conceived of the compulsive repetition of trauma as an effect of the subject's fixation on his or her trauma. To remain fixated on a traumatic experience means that one cannot break free from it, and that one wants to find again the same experience in later years. It was only in 1920 that Freud explained the phenomenon of the compulsion to repeat as a principle property of the drives. In fact, Freud's great discovery that marked a decisive shift in this theory was the finding that the main goal of a drive was not to seek satisfaction or pleasure but to return to an early state of disturbance—a traumatic or healthy state, but one of intense excitation—in order to bring it back and reestablish it in the present. It was this new idea that Freud developed in his text "Beyond the Pleasure Principle." It was *as if*, with this crucial text, the founder of psychoanalysis declared:

> I thought until now that the only goal of the drives was to obtain pleasure, understood as an absence of tension, but I am obliged now to state that the drives often lead the subject to live and relive disturbing childhood emotions, a blend of pleasure and pain. For how would one understand persons who, instead of seeking pleasure, seek to recover unfortunate situations that they already knew and that they were able to avoid? How would one understand someone

who knows full well that a certain behavior has been harmful, but seeks nevertheless to reproduce it, to return to that which made him or her ill? What is this attracting force? No, the drive does not seek exclusively to discharge its tensions and obtain pleasure, but seeks to return to the past, even if a dark one, and to repeat it. I must then, revisit my initial theory and say that the aim of the drives will not be only to gain pleasure but above all to *go back* **and** *to go ahead; to return to find the pregnant past so as to bring it to the present and to repeat it indefinitely.*

Indeed, if we are to imagine the trajectory of a drive, we would draw an arrow that goes forward, then turns back, plunging into the traumatic past, grasping jouissance, and thus charged, continues its progress forward. This takes place many, many times . . . The drives are thus animated by a superior impulse that I refer to as the **principle of repetition**. A drive loves repetition more than the achievement of pleasure. It loves more to turn in a circle than to seek and obtain a goal that is external to it! Also, the principle of repetition operates through a spiraling trajectory of the drive, each of the turns plunging into the unconscious in order to gather the intense past—whether traumatic or not—to deposit it in the present and to relive it.

You will recognize that there is a force in psychical life that is more dominant than our tendency to seek pleasure and avoid distress. This force is a **compulsion to repeat**. To be constrained to externalize the repressed past over and over again is an impulse more irresistible than the impulse to pleasure. What then, would be beyond the pleasure principle, if not the principle of repetition? Freud could well have titled his text "Beyond the Pleasure Principle or the Principle of Repetition." We have thus two principles that act in concert, even if the first is more insistent than the second: the *principle of repetition* that governs the drives in the corridor of time, and the *pleasure principle* that rules their passions.

The motor force of our repetitions, the cause of our impulse to always choose a similar loved one, which leads us to repeat the same manner of loving and suffering with love, the cause that leads us to return unfailingly to the same type of affective attachment, that very cause is the return in the present of a highly exciting and emotionally intense experience.

Before approaching the Lacanian theory of repetition, I would like to raise two central questions for understanding the compulsion to repeat and make some clarifications.

Pathological repetition is *compulsive*; *healthy* repetition is *not compulsive*

➤ *First question: Is the compulsive character of repetition common to all drives or is it one property among others? My response is clear. Influenced as I am by my work with patients, I prefer to reserve the* **compulsive character** *of a drive to the* **death drives** *and maintain, as I develop throughout these pages, that what is proper to* **pathological repetition**—*in contrast to healthy repetition—is that it is* **compulsive**. *We know that for the clinician, this compulsive dimension is common to most psychopathologies.*

➤ *Second question (directly related to the first): Is the "disturbed former state" that the drives seek to re-establish exclusively a traumatic state that rends the ego, or rather can it be a nontraumatic state, however striking, that leaves the ego intact? I have always maintained that the* **disturbed former state, the disturbed childhood past, can be traumatic or non-traumatic.** *If it is* **traumatic** *its active return in the life of the adult will be* **compulsive** *and* **pathological**; *if it is* **non-traumatic** *its active return will be* **non-compulsive** *and* **non-pathological**, *and even agreeable. One comment however, so as to nuance these last affirmations. I do not want the convincing tone of our formulations to*

---

suggest that it is entirely determined in advance and that a young subject affected by a psychical trauma will necessarily be ill as an adult. We know the passion of certain persons can be restored after a traumatic shock.

➤ *I prefer to distinguish repetition of the* **life drives** *(drives of self-preservation and sexual drives) from those of the* **death drives** *(drives of aggression and self-aggression). This distinction corresponds to our two categories of repetition:* **healthy** *and* **pathological.** *The* **life drives** *bring a past to the present that was indeed intense but* **non-traumatic.** *Faithful to their tendency to reunite scattered elements, the life drives integrate the past harmoniously, whether it is forgotten or repressed, into the present reality of the adult subject. The* **death drives,** *on the contrary, bring a past to the present that, more than intense, is* **traumatic.** *True to their tendency to fragment and dissociate coherent elements, the death drives violently impose, in the current reality of the subject, a traumatic, foreclosed, and repressed jouissance, thereby destabilizing the adult subject. This uncontrollable eruption of a jouissance that seeks to remain identical to itself, often takes the form of a personality or behavioral disorder.*

➤ *In addition, I would say that the* **intense** *but* **agreeable past** *acts in the present in the form of* **pleasant behavior** *while the* **traumatic** *and* **painful past** *acts in the present in the form of* **unpleasant** *behavior.*

➤ *The* **intense** *but* **agreeable past** *is a past that can be forgotten or repressed. If it has been simply* **forgotten,** *it could be remembered, and if powerfully exciting it has been repressed, it could actualize itself as a risky choice, an audacious behavior or an ambitious initiative—acts that are certainly prominent but naturally inserted in the normal patterns of the existence of the subject.*

> ➤ *The* **traumatic and painful past** *is a* **foreclosed,** *then* **repressed** *past. Consequently, it can only be actualized as a symptom or as an acting out.*
>
> ### To conclude, here at the two cardinal equations that summarize our theory of healthy and pathological repetition:
>
> ❑ The *non-traumatic* past → Life Drives → *Healthy* and *Non-compulsive* Repetition
> ❑ The *traumatic* past → *Death* Drives → *Pathological* and *Compulsive* Repetition

*

The Lacanian Theory of Repetition:
The Unconscious is Structured as Repetition Automatism[12]

But what is this originary past that the drives gather, animate, and actualize? Following our discussion thus far, we should respond that in the case of pathological repetition it is an unconscious fantasm, and in the case of healthy repetition, it is a quite exciting and affectively intense experience. But in order to approach the Lacanian theory of repetition, I prefer to restrict myself to the fantasm and to its pathological repetition. In fact, strictly speaking, a fantasm cannot be the first originary state that the drives bring to the present, since it is preceded by another fantasm. **A fantasm always issues from the interpretation of a real fact seen through the distorting lens of an even older fantasm.** You recall the case of the child traumatized by the scene of the violence between his or her parents. I considered that the conflict was a real

---

12. See *Seminar on "The Purloined Letter," Écrits*, 6.

fact perceived and registered unconsciously by the child in the form of a fantasmatic scene in which one sees the father's hands strangling the neck of the mother. However, I would like to clarify that the child has interpreted this real fact through a fantasm that already existed in him or her. In fact, the conflict between the mother and the father is seen by the child through the lens of an older fantasm, a fantasm formed since his or her birth and certainly since the Oedipus complex. Another example is that of identical twins who do not experience the same significant fact in the same way since each interprets according to his or her own fantasmatic perception. In other words, every exciting and intensely felt event will be unfailingly perceived, registered, and interpreted though a distorting lens of a preexisting fantasm. Thus, **everything that is affectively important to us is never real but is fantasmatic**. To summarize, we will say that any fantasm is always preceded by another fantasm and that the history of our affective life is a stratification of significant fantasms.

Clearly a fantasm cannot be originary: there is no originary fantasm. The past that the drives gather, carry, and actualize cannot be an inaugural fantasm because a fantasm always refers to another fantasm that supposes another, and yet another, *ad infinitum*. The origin is a discrete point in the infinite depth of the past. This is why the origin that we seek to identify, the originary event that the drives gather, is an immemorial reality that is forever lost, a multifaceted reality that we designate variously as trauma, jouissance, or the real. This is why I propose the following formulation: behind a symptom that is repeated, there is a fantasm that reveals itself; and behind the fantasm there is . . . the real. The real is the enigma of the beginning, but it is also the enigma of the end. In fact, the real is not only the deepest past at the origin of a symptom, it is also its most uncertain future. Seen from a temporal perspective, the real is the twofold enigma of the past and the future, of origin and destiny. Henceforth, if we should respond to the question—"Where is the real situated?"—we would respond: the real is the unknown that frames repetition in the order of time. It is the unknown past and the unknown future. It is the infinite of the past and the infinite of the future. But this is not all. The real is also the thread that links the different moments of repetition. For Lacan, the real is that which always comes back to the same place."[13] But precisely to what place does the real return, if not to that of the Same which repeats itself in the repetitive process? Recall the law of the Same and of the Different. I had told you that the Same is never repeated in a way that is identical to itself, but it is always slightly different, although identifiable as being the same object that returns. In fact, the object of repetition has two dimensions: a core that remains absolutely unchanged—this is the Same—and an envelope that changes with each repetition—this is the Different. Now the real precisely designates the unchanged core of the repetitive object that allows us, in spite of its different appearances, to recognize it as being the same yesterday and today. This is what the thread connects as the moments of repetition: the permanent and timeless core of the Same. We change, but the real within us does not change. This is what we have called the sameness in itself [la mêmeté en soi]. However, we must still recognize that the real corresponds to another agency of which we are already aware: jouissance that is common to the fantasm and to the symptom, and more precisely, the substrate of jouissance. Why the substrate? Because the real is the most intimate core, and the indefinable foundation, of any emotion whatsoever. We have designated this core with the lower case @ in a circle, located within each balloon and in the fantasmatic scene (see figure 2).

If we now translate our remarks into Lacanian terms, we will say that the real is the doubly positioned unknown: in temporal repetition and in topological repetition. In the **temporal** the real is before, after and at the heart of repetition as the core of the Same that remains

---

13. Jacques Lacan, *The Four Fundamental Concepts of Psychoanalysis*, Trans. Alan Sheridan (W. W. Norton & Co., 1981), 49. Hereafter cited as *Four Fundamental Concepts* followed by the page number.

unchanged. In the **topological**, the real is the substrate of jouissance that lies in the fantasm and in the symptom. But if we call the Same of repetition the real, we will call each repetitive occurrence the signifier. What is a signifier? We have already addressed this question, but here I would like to respond differently: a signifier is one of the repetitive occurrences; and the collection of the signifiers is a series of repetitive occurrences forming a signifying chain. Thus if you consider figure 2, each balloon taken in isolation represents a signifier, and the collection of the signifiers materialize the signifying chain. Now, it is necessary to realize that each signifier, as in the case of the others, is the place-holder of the real. In other words, each balloon, each appearance of the same symptom, is the placeholder of the fantasmatic scene. Thus, when Lacan asserts that the real returns always to the same place, we would add that the real returns always to the same place but it does so in the form of the symptom that represents it. Briefly, the real, or *jouissance*, is the Same that appears, disappears, and reappears, each time in the form of a symptom that is slightly different.

In its inexorable event, repetition traverses us and transforms us. But how can we identify this "us" that is modified with each repetitive event? What can we call that which changes in us when we are shaken by the return of our foreclosed and repressed past? Well, what changes in us, that is, the split between what we were before the event of repetition and what we have become after it, is called *the subject*, and more precisely, "the subject of the unconscious." Let us summarize this in the following way. The *real* is the Same before, during, and after the repetitive chain, the inalterable guiding thread that connects the different links of the signifying chain; the *signifier* represents each link of the signifying chain, each repetitive event envisaged as the emergence of the unconscious, of which symptom is the best example; and the *subject of the unconscious* is the split between what we were before the appearance of the signifier and what we become after its appearance. Thus we have the real, the constant of repetition, the signifying *chain* of which each link is a *signifier* similar to the others, and finally *the subject of the unconscious*, which is the effect produced during each repetitive event. It is necessary to add a fourth term to the three terms of the Lacanian algebra of signifier, chain of signifiers, and subject. We have already mentioned it: **objet petit @** is the name given to the real when we locate it at the heart of each repetitive event—the symptom—and at the heart of the unconscious fantasm (figure 2). It can also be said that *Objet petit @* refers to the jouissance that the subject experiences unconsciously in the fantasmatic scene and that it experiences consciously in the symptom.

I would like to make another point about the signifying chain. Previously I had to speak of the role of counting in repetition. In fact, knowing that similar events succeed each other does not allow us to conclude that there is repetition. It requires, you may recall, that someone *counts*. In order to affirm that a symptom repeats itself, it is necessary to turn to the past and count its reoccurrences. It is necessary, then, to count in order for repetition to exist. When Rachel tells me—"That has been going on long time. My first crises appeared just before I was twenty; then I forgot them only to experience them again at the time of my meeting with Jerome; and then the month that I came to Paris, I was again overcome"—what occurs if not the itemization of her sorrows. Each time the crisis is slightly different, but the *jouissance* remains the same: distress, distress, distress. . . .

In order to conclude my reading of the concept of repetition in Lacan's work I would like to recall the terms of Lacan's algebra and offer a definition of the unconscious from the perspective of repetition. The Lacanian algebra is represented in the following way: • S_1 indicates the signifier$_1$, that is to say the repetitive event on the basis of which I deduce that it is the last link in a repetitive chain that began before it and that will continue after it. • S_2 indicates the entirety of signifiers, that is to say, the chain of repetitive events or signifying chain. • $ indicates the subject of the unconscious, that is to say, the effect of repetitive action. Finally, @ indicates the *object petit a* that symbolizes the presence of jouissance as in the fantasized scene as in

THE FOUR LAWS OF REPETITION	• Real (Same)/ Symbolic (Different) • Presence/Absence • The human agent who counts the repetitions (the analyst) • The human agent constituted by repetition
WHAT IS REPEATED?	What is repeated is a jouissance that is foreclosed, repressed and encapsulated in a fantasmatic scene
THE NUMBER OF TIMES WHERE JOUISSANCE IS REPEATED?	Each reappearance of jouissance in the form of a symptom, is a signifier; and the series of reappearances are the chain of signifiers
THE PURPOSE OF REPETITION	• The compulsive repetition of jouissance is an automatisme that has no other purpose than to continue to repeat itself • The only purpose of repetition is to produce an effect: *the subject of the unconscious*

Diagram 1. Repetition According to Lacan

the symptom. Considered in their synergy these four terms institute a movement known as **repetition** *automatism.* The term *"automatism"* designates the machine-like automatic functioning of a limited, driven unconscious, whose only goal is to blindly follow its path in three moments: to seek *jouissance* in the past, to bring it to the surface, and to project it ahead, pressuring it to begin again. More simply, the only purpose of the unconscious is to persist by virtue of repetition. All of these considerations lead us to understand unconscious action. Our life is determined by repetitive eruptions of the unconscious. I would like to recall the well-known Lacanian aphorism "the unconscious is structured like a language" and propose the following formulation: *The unconscious is structured by repetition automatism.* More synthetically I will conclude that: **The unconscious is repetition!**

*

An Example of Pathological Repetition:
Bernard, or the Uncontrollable and
Repetitive Need to be Humiliated

I would like to share the case of Bernard with you, a case that is an eloquent illustration of a pathological repetition. This case that Freud would have called a "fate neurosis" [*Schicksalneurose*] and that I prefer to identify as a "neurosis of compulsive repetition" [*névrose de répétition compulsive*], is also an example of the therapeutic capacity of the transference to stop an unbearable repetition.

Bernard was unable to marry. This 35-year-old civil servant came to see me after three successive engagements failed, all failures having occurred only hours before the marriage ceremony. The same scenario happened each time: invaded by doubt, overcome by panic, he fled and left everything behind: fiancé, family, invited guests, and even the justice of the peace. Besides the numerous difficulties caused by these disconcerting about-faces, Bernard consulted me because he remained alone and despaired at the idea of never being able to have a family. In the course of his therapy, two other symptoms appeared that were just as compulsive, symptoms which led me to gradually reconstruct the unconscious and toxic fantasmatic scene at the origin of his neurosis. I can say immediately that thanks to this reconstruction of the fantasm, we—the patient and analyst—were able to interpret the different disturbances, and were able, toward the end of the analysis, to prepare the occurrence of the crucial ordeal of revivification. In this way we were able to bring the morbid repetition to an end.

Bernard completed his analysis some years ago and I was pleased recently to receive the announcement of the birth of his second child. I do not hesitate to tell you that this was a successful analysis with a favorable outcome. Happily for our patients and for we analysts, many analyses conclude very positively after a process that is sometimes long, and sometimes perhaps less long, often difficult but always exciting. I am sharing the case of Bernard with you, not only because it illustrates the two modalities of pathological repetition that we just studied (temporal and topological), but also because it is the best way to show the course of therapeutic action for a psychoanalyst when confronted with repetition compulsion.

In order to complete the clinical picture of our patient, I can tell you that besides the successive ruptures of his engagements, Bernard suffered from two other compulsions that provided him with pleasure and pain simultaneously. First, he had the habit of masturbating while on a phone sex line, while a demeaning and abusive feminine voice ordered him to get down on his hands and knees and to imagine himself being beaten, soiled, and sodomized by a dominant woman. For him, this was the only way to have an orgasm. Once he achieved the release, he immediately regretted having given in once again to the abject and irrepressible desire to seek pleasure in such humiliation. The second activity, which was just as compulsive, was that he went each week, for four hours, to the other end of France, to be in the chair of dentist's office, open his mouth, and endure the painful treatments of his own father, a dental surgeon nearing retirement.

With a compulsive need to break his engagements, a compulsive need to masturbate while humiliating himself, and a compulsive need to be mistreated by his father, Bernard lived in the grasp of an immaterial drug known as "jouissance," a blend of excitation, voluptuousness, pain, shame, and self-contempt. He was unable to prevent himself from seeking this state of quivering with desire when, for example, he prepared for his masturbation ritual and felt the excitation rise, an excitation that culminated in the phone sex abuse, and diminished immediately in a disappointing ejaculation. Once the ceremony was concluded, the excitation returned in a profound self-disgust.

But why this uncontrollable and repetitive need to be cursed by his fiancés and their families, humiliated by the voice on the telephone, and mistreated by a sadistic father? To what invisible and diabolical master was Bernard enslaved? Bernard was the slave of *jouissance* because he lived under the domination of an unconscious fantasm that was obstinately eager to be externalized. As I just mentioned, it was on the basis of the three compulsive needs—to flee, to masturbate, and to surrender to the father—that I was led to understand that the fantasm by which Bernard was plagued was a unique childhood scene in which he incarnates all the characters. It was a scene that he played and replayed constantly, without his knowledge and to his detriment. What scene? It is impossible here to recall all the moments of this case. I will limit myself to only evoking a painful memory I have already mentioned as an example of psychical trauma. In this painful memory, mentioned several times in the session, Bernard, as a child, was the disturbed witness of unbearable disputes during which his father insulted and savagely struck his mother. On the basis of this memory and on the basis of the three compulsive needs that we have discussed, I theoretically reconstructed a scene that I supposed to be the unconscious scene at the origin of the neurosis of Bernard's repetition compulsion. I assumed that little Bernard was not limited to seeing his parents fight in this memory. In the reconstructed scene, the little boy plays all the roles simultaneously, that of the tormenter, that of the victim, and that of the witness: he is at the same time the one who strikes, the one who screams, and he himself, the stunned spectator. At times Bernard takes the position of the father's sadism, at times of the humiliation of the mother, and at times the stupefaction of the witness; each of these feelings is mixed with rage against the aggressive father, and the urge to take action to defend his mother.

I mentioned that this was a successful treatment since the series of repetitions was fortunately interrupted. It is always difficult to treat a neurosis of repetition compulsion. Also, I would like to share the psychical exchanges between analyst and patient with you, exchanges that facilitated the successful treatment. A preliminary remark: we must understand that to put an end to a chain of repetitions it is above all, necessary that the analytic relation involve a theatrical staging, including the analyst, of a new neurosis called "transference neurosis." Indeed, if the patient is strongly attached, neurotically, to his or her analyst, to the point of loving him or her—not without ambivalence—in the same way he loved one of his parents, he becomes open and receptive to the therapist's interventions. In this way, the therapist is also closer to his patient. This reciprocal trust places the analyst in the best position to facilitate a unique identification that will allow him or her to not only intellectually reconstruct the fantasmatic scene, but also to perceive it emotionally. Thus, I identified myself with the little Bernard, and I re-enacted within me the same fantasmatic jouissance caused by stupefaction, sadism, humiliation, and the revulsion experienced by the child disturbed by the violence of the scene. I would like to be clear. I did not identify myself with the adult patient on the couch. Of course I was sensitive to the emotions that animated his speech, but it was not the conscious emotions that I was specifically seeking to revive. When the identification with the little Bernard happened, the psychoanalyst identified himself with an imaginary creature that he forged in his mind, and felt what it would feel if it existed. And what would it feel, if not simultaneously, but the fury of the father, the degradation of the mother, and the stupefaction of the one who witnessed the scene? Clearly that imaginary child was not a reverie born in the floating attention; on the contrary, it was the outcome of an extremely concentrated listening, a listening nourished by the knowledge of the patient, his history, and his resistances and suffering.

On the strength of this identification I was able to show my analysand, when he could accept it, that the compulsive disturbances of today result from the toxic action of the fantasmatic scene enclosed in his unconscious. Here is one example of my interventions. I was able to reveal to Bernard that to masturbate while being insulted was a way of reliving the humiliation of the mother subjected to the blows of the father. Getting down on his hands and knees while wielding a dildo, he took the place of the humiliated mother; while the dominating and insulting voice on the telephone—that of a woman—translated the degrading contempt of the father. Thus interpreted many times, the unconscious scene gradually became a scene that was consciously recognized. From a painful memory we have passed to the fantasmatic unconscious scene, and then to that of the scene understood consciously. I just wrote: "interpreted many times," and I already hear the objections advanced by some of our patients when they complain that their analysis "goes in circles." But it is necessary to go in a circle! It is necessary to reconsider the same themes, but differently each time, to encounter the same questions again, finding, in the end, a way out. There is always a way out! In the end, each of our patients—and each of us—gravitates around two or three wounds that, often opened in childhood or adolescence, become constant thorns in our hearts. In addition, analysis can only relentlessly return to our eternal blindness and wounds. I say one must not hesitate to interpret, more than once, the same unconscious scene and to try, gradually, to bring it to consciousness in the patient. It is only in this way that we will see the compulsive repetition subside and give way to another form of repetition, one that is healthy: the revivification of the jouissance of the traumatic scene. This is the richest and most delicate experience of the therapeutic process that I also call the moment of emotional awareness.

It is thus that Bernard experienced sessions where he rediscovered the jouissance of his fantasm in my presence. But before describing this eminently therapeutic experience of revivification, I would like to address once again the analyst's interpretation, without which the revivification could not take place. One of the errors that young practitioners often commit is of believing that it is sufficient to explain to the patient what he or she has not understood in order to achieve the resolution of his or her suffering. A novice practitioner mistakenly thinks that the essence of psychoanalysis involves the transmission of conscious knowledge to the patient. This is not the case. What is crucial is not the transmission of knowledge, even if correct, but rather the manner of the transmission. What is important is to evoke the emotion in the patient that is attuned to the speech of the analyst as if it were his or her own, as if he or she were addressing it to him- or herself, as if his or her consciousness received the message from the unconscious. In order to actualize this genuine effect it is also necessary that the therapist—while separating one's personal life from one's professional activity—be also caught up by the emotion and utterance of simple and moving words. These are words that cause the resistance of the ego to weaken and allow unconscious jouissance to make its way directly to consciousness. This moment, when the analyst's moving words are met by a silence that is just as moving from the patient [analysand], constitutes one of the events unique to analysis. It is an event that announces the occurrence of the subsequent experience of the revivification that we will now address.

*

Psychoanalytic Treatment of Pathological Repetition through its Revivification

Now we will approach revivification, which is the other form of repetition. Thus far, I have distinguished three modes of returning to the past: the conscious return, or re-memoration, the act or actualization of return in healthy acts, and the return in pathological acts. There is still another modality of actualization of unconscious repression, which is no longer compulsive but prepared for and expected by the therapist, namely the revivification of traumatic jouissance, a revivification induced by the psychoanalyst and conditioned by the transference. This is exactly what was experienced by Bernard, when after numerous interpretations that had relaxed his ego and rendered his dialogue within himself more fluid, in the course of a limited number of intense and at times painful sessions, he experienced the jouissance proper to his own fantasm of humiliation, which until then had not been felt. Now, the therapeutic goal of an analysis is precisely to **neutralize the toxic childhood fantasm** or, if you prefer, to **gradually dissolve compulsive jouissance**. How do we proceed? By accomplishing three decisive steps. If these steps occur, one can be certain that the cure will proceed positively toward its conclusion.

With the first step, we lead the patient to re-experience the unconscious traumatic situation within the analytic scene. He or she enters into the state of revivification where the analysand feels and perceives in him- or herself the jouissance inherent to the unconscious fantasm. From the case of Bernard you have understood well that it is not simply a case of a re-memoration. To support **the revivification of** past **emotion** is very different from the **evocation** of a painful **memory**. One involves a *revivification* through which the patient experiences the jouissance of the fantasm vitally and psychically—a jouissance that had until then never been consciously felt. The other involves being affected by the evocation of a painful event. I note that the **revivification is not a sudden experience** that happens just once, it happens over the course of several successive sessions as a result of analytic preparation. Let me be more precise. What does it mean concretely to experience the jouissance of one's fantasm? Revivification is not just the eruption of a feeling, it is also the consciousness of being affected by that feeling. It is necessary to simultaneously **feel again** and **to be conscious of feeling again, to differentiate between the one who relives the trauma and the one sees him- or herself relive the trauma**. This moment of the self-perception of the analysand calls, on the part of the analyst, for a stance that renders him or her a silent witness of a genuine revelation on the basis of which the patient discovers the feelings experienced by the characters of his or her fantasm.

When the analysand and the analyst cross this overwhelming moment of reliving repressed emotion, they share an exceptional human encounter. However, going through these privileged moments is not sufficient to fully relieve the patient of the morbid fantasms. This must be accompanied by a speech capable of giving a meaning to the return of the buried past. Now that the repressed resurges with all its emotional intensity, words must name it and inscribe it in a narrative, words enunciated by the analyst and at times by the patient. It is less important who pronounces the words. What matters is that if one succeeds in naming the painful emotion that is reborn, it can be integrated into the ego of the subject, and with time it will dissipate.

With the second step, the analysand gradually becomes aware of the traumatic past. At the same time, he or she acquires an insight **gathered from** his or her current behavior.

In the third and final step, in a similar way that the work of mourning allows the one who mourns to gradually detach him- or herself from the loved one who was lost, the repetition of the revivification allows the analysand to gradually identify less with the characters in his or her fantasm and to withdraw from the emotions experienced by those characters. In mourning, the one who mourns becomes detached from the loved one who has been lost. In the process of revivification the analysand becomes detached from a toxic jouissance that alienates him or her.

*

To conclude with the theme of revivification I would like to define the position of the psychoanalyst in relation to the unconscious *ego* that represses, and in relation to the unconscious *id* that, on the contrary, directs all of its forces to succeed in activating jouissance again in compulsive and unpredictable behavior. Thus I would distinguish between the attitude of the **id**, the **ego**, and the **psychoanalyst**. Here are their reactions to a psychological trauma from childhood:

- ❐ The id has only one goal: to do everything to lead the traumatic jouissance into the light of day so that it vibrates in the adult body and it breaks out in an impulsive action.

- ❐ The ego, on the other hand, which no longer wants to suffer, wants to know nothing of the horrible trauma, whether in memory or in action. It represses it desperately.

- ❐ And finally, the psychoanalyst, also wants the id to drive the traumatic jouissance, not in a violent or compulsive action, but through a gradual revivification that is serene and articulated; and, in the same hope of advancing the cure, he or she would also like the ego be less feeble and not fear memory of the trauma. For the psychoanalyst, the savage action of the id is a resistance similar to the ferocious resistance of the ego.

The **ego** engages in **repression** because it is afraid to remember the trauma; while the **id** engages in **repetition compulsion** because it savors the trauma and wants to experience it again. In a word, repression is an "I no longer want to know!" while the repetition is an "I want it again!"

*

Now, I would like to conclude this chapter by sharing two voices with you, voices that resonate in unison, and address the same message to us. The first is a timeless voice that teaches us that the past never disappears despite the passage of time and that it can always return.

Once deeds are done, whether in justice or contrary to it, not even Time, the father of all, could undo their outcome.[14]

The other voice, which is more contemporary, resonates with Pindar, adding that the past is not only ineffaceably present but that it is active within us. Insofar as we are alive, it will constantly be reflected in our conscience and in our actions.

"In mental life nothing that has once been formed can perish—everything is somehow preserved and . . . can once more be brought to light."[15]

The first quotation emanates from an ancient thinker who lived in Thebes five centuries before our era. It is the voice of Pindar, an unequalled master of universal poetry. The second, you already know, is the voice of another master, more present than ever among us, Sigmund Freud. More than two thousand years apart these voices confirm the same truth that I would formulate in the following way: *Everything that is vital to us today is a repetition of what has already been.* This is the truth that must orient the practitioner when we listen to a patient who shares his or her illness with us. By listening to his or her distress, we know spontaneously that what he or she experiences today is clearly the repetition of what has been experienced in the past.

*

14. Pindar, *Olympian Odes, Pythian Odes*, ed. and trans. William H. Race, Loeb Classical Library 56 (Cambridge, MA: Harvard University Press, 1997), 65.

15. "Civilization and Its Discontents," SE XXI, 69.

	Healthy Repetition	Pathological Compulsive Repetition	Therapeutic Revivification
The Three Laws of Repetition	• The Same/The Different • Presence/Absence • A human agent who counts repetitions	• The Same/The Different • Presence/Absence • A human agent who counts repetitions	Revivification entails the return of traumatic jouissance in the course of the cure, in the form of a vivid emotion that is felt again by an analysand who is capable of distinguishing between the one who relives the trauma and the one who sees him or herself relive the trauma
The Effects of Repetition	Beneficial Effects • Self-Preservation • Self-fulfillment • Affirmation of our identity in the course of time	Pathologies of Repetition • Inexplicable repetition of our errors and our failures • Imperious need to constantly replay again an infantile traumatic experience without knowing it • A man who multiplies romantic break ups, since he fails to find the ideal woman (his mother) • Obsessive Compulsive Disturbances • Addictive behavior (drugs, gambling, bulimia, sexual perversions, delinquency)	

	Healthy Repetition	Pathological Compulsive Repetition	Therapeutic Revivification
The return of the past in the present	• Rememoration is the return to consciousness or a _forgotten_ past. • Healthy repetition is the return, in our behavior, of a repressed past * • The unconscious is a life force that amplifies our being	Pathological Repetition is the compulsive return in our symptoms and in our acting out of a traumatic, foreclosed, and repressed past * The unconscious is a force of death that impels the subject to ceaselessly re-experience the same sensual, and traumatically painful jouissance	Revivification is not a sudden experience that occurs only once. It happens over the course of several successive sessions and after a period of analytic preparation. Revivification shows us that the process of healing has begun.
What is repeated?	What is repeated is our troubled and repressed past	What is repeated is the traumatic jouissance encapsulated in an unconscious fantasmatic scene	
What is the motor force of repetition?	The motor force of repetition is the drive. Instead of seeking to alleviate its tension and obtain pleasure, the drive prefers to guard its tension and lead jouissance to tirelessly repeat itself		

Diagram 2. Summary: ☐Healthy repetition ☐Pathological Compulsive Repetition ☐Therapeutic Revivification

2.

Excerpts from Freud and Lacan on Repetition, Preceded by Our Commentaries

Freud

One always returns to the first loves

Love today is always the repetition of the prototype of the first childhood love for the mother. To love is invariably to love for the second time. However, let us not oversimplify this: love is never a simple repetition of the love for the mother. Innumerable psychical events since our birth render our adult love complex, unique and mysterious. J.-D. N.

"*On revient toujours à ses premiers amours*" is a sober truth.[1]

*

---

1. "The Claims of Psycho-analysis to Scientific Interest," SE XIII, 183. TN. In French in the original.

"There are good reasons why a child sucking at his mother's breast has become the prototype of every relation of love. **The finding of an object is in fact the refinding of it.**"[2]

*

Because it is the reissue of a first childhood love, love is marked by this compulsion proper to all that emanates from the unconscious. I am convinced that love is such an imperious drive that we cannot not love. To love is a vital need that must continuously be satisfied by an object, whether a human being, an animal, an ideal, or itself. What is important is to love! J.-D. N.

"Love consists of new **editions** of old traits and that it **repeats** infantile reactions. But this is the essential character of every state of being in love. There is no such state that does not reproduce infantile prototypes. It is precisely from this infantile determination that it receives its **compulsive character**, verging as it does on the pathological."[3]

*

IN LIFE THERE ARE TWO TYPES OF REPETITION:
A MANAGEABLE, HEALTHY REPETITION THAT GIVES US
STRUCTURE AND REASSURANCE; AND AN UNMANAGEABLE,
PATHOLOGICAL REPETITION THAT CAUSES US TO SUFFER

Repetition can gain us pleasure (for example, the child is happy to always find his or her favorite game), or cause

---

2. "Three Essays on Sexuality," SE VII, 222.

3. "Observations on Transference-Love," SE XII, 168.

us to suffer (for example, to regularly experience the same failure). Repetition is healthy when it can be managed, and pathological repetition is compulsive and unmanageable. J.-D. N.

"But children will never tire of asking an adult to repeat a game that he has shown them or played with them, till he is too exhausted to go on. And if a child has been told a nice story, he will insist on hearing it over and over again instead of a new one; and he will remorselessly stipulate that the repetition should be an identical one.

. . . None of this contradicts the principle of repetition; **repetition, the re-experiencing of something identical, is clearly in itself a source of pleasure.** In the case of a person in analysis, on the contrary, the compulsion to repeat the events of his childhood in the transference evidently disregards the pleasure principle in every way."[4] Freud

*

The sudden and compulsive eruption of the repressed causes us to suffer (symptom), but is also a discharge of tension that relieves us. It is both a suffering for the conscious ego and a relief for the unconscious id. This apparent contradiction disappears with the Lacanian concept of jouissance, since jouissance is as painful as it is pleasurable. J.-D. N.

"It is clear that the greater part of what is re-experienced under the compulsion to repeat must cause the ego unpleasure, since it brings to light activities of repressed instinctual

---

4. "Beyond the Pleasure Principle," SE XVIII, 35–36.

impulses. That, however, is unpleasure of a kind we have already considered and does not contradict the pleasure principle: unpleasure for one system and simultaneously satisfaction for the other."[5] Freud

*

THE MISFORTUNE THAT SEEMS TO HAUNT CERTAIN PERSONS LED FREUD TO PROPOSE THE CONCEPT OF THE COMPULSION TO REPEAT

After having been subjected to a series of unfortunate events, the subject believes itself to be the victim of fatalism, while in truth, it is him or herself who, in all innocence, repetitively provokes these successive problems. The subject is unaware that, during each event, he or she compulsively replays an ancient childhood fantasm in the form of a behavioral failure. J.-D. N.

The impression they give [normal people] is of being pursued by a malignant fate or possessed by some 'daemonic' power; but psychoanalysis has always taken the view that their fate is for the most part arranged by themselves. . . .[6] Freud

*

"There are people in whose lives the same reactions are perpetually being repeated uncorrected, to their own detriment, or others who seem to be pursued by a relentless

---

5. "Beyond the Pleasure Principle," SE XVIII, 20.

6. Ibid., 21.

fate, though closer investigation teachers us that they are unwittingly bringing this fate on themselves. In such cases we attribute a 'daemonic' character to the **compulsion to repeat**."[7] Freud

*

THE TRANSFERENCE IS AN EXAMPLE OF REPETITION IN
ACTION IN WHICH SOMETHING THAT HAS BEEN REPRESSED
SURFACES IN THE BEHAVIOR OF THE ANALYSAND
IN RELATION TO THE PSYCHOANALYST

A forgotten event can rise in consciousness as a memory. In the case that the event has been not only forgotten, but energetically repressed, it resurges as an emotion or a form of behavior that the subject commits without know that it enacts the repressed. Instead of a memory, it is a matter of a repressed past.

In the passage you will read, Freud uses two terms inter-changeably: "forgotten" and "repressed." However, I believe it is better to establish a distinction. While the forgotten event rises from the preconscious to consciousness, the repressed event, having been subjected to the strong pressure of cen-sorship, springs from the unconscious and takes the form of an action. Consciousness does not resist the return of the forgotten, although it is fiercely opposed to the return of the repressed. J.-D. N.

"We may say that the patient does not *remember* anything of what he has forgotten and represented, but *acts* it out.

---

7. "New Introductory Lectures on Pscyho-Analysis," SE XXII, 106–07.

He reproduces it not as a memory but as an action; he *repeats* it, without, of course, knowing that he is repeating it."[8] Freud

*

"The patient cannot remember the whole of what is repressed in him, and what he cannot remember may be precisely the essential of it. . . . He is obliged to *repeat* the repressed material as a contemporary experience instead of, as the physician would prefer to see, remembering it as something belonging to the past."[9] Freud

*

Freud proposes two examples of the transference considered as repetition that enacts the repressed. The first example involves a patient that is insolent in relation to the analyst, instead of remembering that he or she had been insolent in relation to his or her parents. A second example involves a patient who declares to his analyst that he or she has nothing to say instead of remembering that as a child he or she had wanted to seduce the father by being silent and submissive. In these two examples, the patient does not remember the repressed fact but enacts it in the analytic scene. This is repetition in action! J.-D. N.

"For instance, the patient does not say that he remembers that he used to be defiant and critical towards his parents' authority; instead, he behaves in that way to the doctor."

---

8. "Remembering, Repeating, and Working-Through," SE XII, 150.

9. "Beyond the Pleasure Principle," SE XVIII, 18.

... [When asked] to say what occurs to his mind, one expects him to poor out a flood of information; but often the first thing that happens is that he has nothing to say. He is silent and declares that nothing occurs to him. This, of course, is merely a **repetition** of a homosexual attitude which comes to the fore as a resistance against remembering anything. As long as the patient is in the treatment he cannot escape from this **compulsion to repeat**; and in the end we understand that this is his way of remembering.

... We soon perceive that the transference is itself only a **piece of repetition**, and that **repetition is a transference of the forgotten past.** . . ."[10] Freud

*

THE TRANSFERENCE CAN STOP REPETITION COMPULSION AND TRANSFORM IT INTO MEMORY

The attachment of the analysand to the psychoanalyst is due to a transference of feelings onto the person of the therapist (repetition in action) The practitioner uses the transference to revive repetitively—in the analysand—the jouissance experienced during a childhood trauma. J.-D. N.

The main instrument . . . for **curbing the patient's compulsion to repeat** and for turning it into a motive for remembering lies in the handling of the transference. We render the compulsion harmless, and indeed useful, by giving it the right to assert itself in a definite field. We admit it into the transference as a playground in which it is allowed

---

10. Ibid., 150–51.

to expand in almost complete freedom and in which it is expected to display to us everything in the way of pathogenic instincts that is hidden in the patient's mind.[11] Freud

*

THE REPEATED REVIVIFICATION OF TRAUMATIC JOUISSANCE DISSOLVES IT AND ALLOWS THE ANALYSAND TO GAIN INSIGHT ON HIS OR HER SITUATION. IN ADDITION, THE REPEATED REVIVIFICATION IS EQUIVALENT TO THE WORK OF MOURNING.

"Recollection without affect almost invariably produces no result. The psychical process which originally took place must be repeated as vividly as possible; it must be brought back to its *status nascendi* and then given verbal utterance."[12] Freud

*

". . . **an analysis falls into two clearly distinguishable phases**. In the **first**, the physician procures from the patient the necessary information, makes him familiar with the premises and postulates of psycho-analysis, and unfolds to him the reconstruction of the genesis of his disorder as deduced from the materials brought up in the analysis. In the **second** phase the patient himself gets hold of the material put before him; he works on it, recollects what he can of the apparently repressed memories, and tries to repeat the rest as if he were in some way **living it over again**."[13] Freud

---

11. Ibid., 154.

12. "Studies on Hysteria," SE II, 6.

13. "The Psychogenesis of Case of Homosexuality in a Woman," SE XVIII, 152.

*

The principle of repetition is more powerful than the pleasure principle

There is a more powerful force in psychical life than our ten-dency to seek pleasure and avoid unpleasure. The pressure of repression that seeks to manifest itself in a symptom or in an action repetitively, is a force that is more irresistible than the search for pleasure. J.-D. N.

". . . there really does exist in the mind a compulsion to repeat which overrides the pleasure principle."[14] Freud

*

The principal goal of a drive is to go back in order to bring the disturbed past to the present

Freud's great discovery, in 1920, that marked a decisive shift in his work, was of understanding that the goal of the drive was not to seek pleasure as much as to return to an earlier state of being disturbed so as to bring it back and re-establish it in the present. If we should imagine the trajectory of a drive we would draw an arrow that would fly forward, then turn back to become transformed and charged, and then resume its path to the present. This would happen repetitively. J.-D. N.

"For they [*the Instincts*] reveal an effort to restore an earlier state of things. We may suppose that from the moment at which the state of things that has once been attained

---

14. "Beyond the Pleasure Principle," SE XVIII, 22.

is upset, an instinct arises to create it afresh and brings about phenomena which we can describe as a 'compulsion to repeat.' "[15] Freud

*

". . . the organic instincts are conservative, are acquired historically and tend towards the restoration of an earlier state of things.[16] Freud

*

"But how is the predicate of being 'instinctual' related to the compulsion to repeat? . . . *It seems that an instinct is an urge inherent in organic life to restore an earlier state of things* which the living entity has been obliged to abandon under the pressure of disturbing external forces; that is, it is a kind of organic elasticity.[17] Freud

*

"**Instinct** in general is regarded as a kind of elasticity of living things, an impulse towards the **restoration of a situation which once existed** but was brought to an end by some external disturbance. This essentially conservative character of instincts is exemplified by the phenomena of the *compulsion to repeat*."[18] Freud

---

15. New Introductory Lectures, SE XXII, 106.

16. "Beyond the Pleasure Principle," SE XVIII, 37–38.

17. "Beyond the Pleasure Principle," SE XVIII, 36.

18. "An Autobiographical Study," SE XX, 57.

*

What is the object that is repeated?

The object that is repeated is a childhood fantasm charged with a foreclosed and repressed jouissance, a fantasm isolated within the unconscious and pressured to breach the barrier of censorship in order to erupt in the life of the subject in the form of a symptom, conflictual behavior and or an unfortunate choice. J.-D. N.

We have learned that the patient repeats instead of remembering, and repeats under the conditions of resistance. We may ask what it is that he in fact repeats or acts out. The answer is that he repeats everything that has already made its way from the sources of the repressed into his manifest personality.[19] Freud

*

Insofar as it is not rendered symbolic and integrated into the ego, jouissance surges compulsively

Any jouissance that is foreclosed, isolated and loose in the unconscious, seeks to manifest itself compulsively in the life of the subject in the form of an action or a symptom. Put differently, any compulsion to repeat is triggered by a jouissance that burns to be heard. It is as if a jouissance that is not rendered symbolic or not represented was a wild horse that only a word from the analyst could calm. From the moment

---

19. "Remembering, Repeating, and Working Through," SE XII, 160.

*that the therapist finds a meaning for the symptom, that is
to say, reveals to the analysand the fantasmatic scene whose
symptom is the expression, jouissance is integrated into the
ego, calmed, ceases to be repeated and the symptom disappears. J.-D. N.*

"The repressed is now, as it were, an outlaw; it is excluded
from the great organization of the ego and is subject only to
the laws that govern the realm of the unconscious."[20] Freud

*

THE ONE WHO DOES NOT KNOW HIS OR HER PAST
IS CONDEMNED TO SEE IT RETURN IN THE FORM OF AN
IMPULSIVE BEHAVIOR OR A FAILURE

*Here is a passage where Freud enunciates one of the main
principles of psychoanalysis: the person who does not know
the origin of his or her suffering is condemned to see it
repeated. Inversely, knowing the origin of our suffering is
the only remedy for preventing its repetition. I cannot resist
recalling here a sentence from Spinoza that reflects this thesis:*
**"An emotion, which is a passion ceases to be passion, as
we form a clear and distinct idea thereof."**[21] *Psychoanalytically speaking, I would have said pathogenic jouissance
ceases to be, as soon as we have repetitively re-experienced
it like mourning and in the context of the transference. That
being the case, the Freudian principle in question, that we can
read in the next passage, can be summarized in the following*

---

20. "Inhibitions, Symptoms and Anxiety," SE XX, 153.

21. *The Chief Works of Benedict de Spinoza*, V. II, The Ethics, Part V, PROP. III,
trans. R. H. M. Elwes (New York: Dover Publications, 1951), 248.

way: what has not been interpreted and remains unknown, always remains.

Let us note that in the first lines of the passage below, Freud establishes a distinction that is very useful to listening more effectively to our patients: it is one thing to simply hear the story of a dream, for example, and another thing to interpret it, that is to say to explain unconscious desire that is generating the dream to the patient. J.-D. N.

"Unluckily, his father failed to interpret either of these phantasies, so that Hans himself gained nothing from telling them." Freud adds that the absence of interpretation leads to repetition: "a thing which has not been understood, inevitably reappears; like an unlaid ghost, it cannot rest until the mystery has been solved and the spell broken."[22] Freud

*

WHY DO WE NOT FORGET, ONCE AND FOR ALL,
A TRAUMATIC EVENT? WHY DOES IT RETURN OBSTINATELY
IN OUR SLEEP AND CAUSE US ANXIETY?

Here is Freud's response: the trauma reappears in our nightmares in order to allow us to experience anxiety that was absent during the traumatic experience. If there was a trauma, it was because the subject, instead of experiencing anxiety, was paralyzed by fear and stupefied. To want to relive the trauma is to seek to replace the paralyzing fear with anxiety; the passive attitude of the victim with the active attitude of anxiety. It is as if the traumatized subjectunfailingly

---

22. "Analysis of a Phobia in a Five-Year-Old Boy," SE X, 122.

reproduces the traumatic scene in order to complete it, rectify, and master it. J.-D. N.

"The ego, which experienced the trauma passively, now repeats it actively. . . ."[23] Freud

*

"These dreams [by their repetitive character] are endeavouring to master the stimulus retrospectively, by developing the anxiety whose omission was the cause of the traumatic neurosis."[24] Freud

*

We distinguish two modes of functioning of pathological repetition: **a temporal repetition** *and a* **topological repetition**. *In the case of* **temporal** *repetition, the symptom is repeated several times on a time line; and in the case of* **topological** *repetition, the symptom repeats and manifests the unconscious fantasm. J.-D. N.*

"If the philosophers maintain that the concepts of space and time are the necessary forms of our thinking, forethought tells us that the individual masters the world by means of two systems, one of which functions only in terms of time and the other only in terms of space."[25] Freud

---

23. "Inhibitions, Symptoms and Anxiety," SE XX, 167.

24. "Beyond the Pleasure Principle," SE XVIII, 32.

25. "129 Scientific Meeting on February 1, 1911," in *Minutes of the Vienna Psychoanalytic Society*, Volume III: 1910–1911, trans. M. Nunberg (New York: International Universities Press, Inc., 1974), 149.

*

The neurosis in the child [the Oedipus complex] often remains overlooked and is not discovered until much later, in adulthood, in the form of a new neurosis. In truth, any adult neurosis repeats a childhood neurosis. J.-D. N.

"If a neurosis breaks out in later life, analysis regularly reveals it as a direct continuation [*la repetition*] of the infantile illness which may have emerged as no more than a veiled hint."[26] Freud

*

Lacan

For Lacan, the human being is not the agent of repetition, he or she is its product

Lacan has formalized the Freudian notion of the compulsion to repeat with the concept of the signifying chain: each link of the chain represents a repetitive occurrence. Also, repetition is a sequence of signifiers, an insistence of the signifying chain to say the unsayable real. J.-D. N.

"My research has led me to the realization that repetition automatism [*Wiederholungzwang*] has its basis in what I have called the insistence of the signifying chain."[27] Lacan

---

26. "Introductory Lectures on Psycho-Analysis," SE XVI, 364.

27. *Seminar on "The Purloined Letter," Écrits*, 6.

Like a recurrent symptom, the signifier is repeated in an alternating rhythm of appearances and disappearances. J.-D. N.

"For we have learned to conceive of the signifier as sustaining itself only in a **displacement** comparable to that found in electronic news strips. . . . This is because of the alternating operation at its core that requires it to leave its place, if only to return to it by a circular path." (our emphasis)[28] Lacan

*The compulsion to repeat determines not only the subjectivity of the subject, but also the intersubjectivity among several subjects; for example, within a family, between a father and his daughter, or even between a grandfather and his grandson. This is what we refer to as **transgenerational repetition**. J.-D. N.*

"The signifier's displacement determines subject's acts, destiny, refusals, blindnesses, success and fate. . . ."[29] Lacan

". . . the subject follows the channels of the symbolic. But what is illustrated here is more gripping still: It is not only the subject, but the subjects, caught in their intersubjectivity, who line up . . . and who more docile than sheep, model their very being on the moment of the signifying chain that runs through them."[30] Lacan

---

28. *Écrits*, 21.

29. Ibid.

30. Ibid.

The Unconscious is Structured Like Repetition **Automatism**. J.-D. N.

"This enables us to grasp by what means the order of the unconscious appears. To what does Freud refer it? What is its surety? It is what he succeeds, in a second stage, in resolving by elaborating the function of repetition."[31] Lacan

Behind a symptom that is repeated, there is a fantasm that actualizes itself; and behind the fantasm there is the real. In the beginning was the real. By using the vocabulary of our book, I would say, behind a symptom that is repeated, there is a fantasm that actualizes itself; and, embedded in the fantasm, simmers the traumatic jouissance, the knot of the real. In the beginning was the real of traumatic jouissance. J.-D. N.

"If you wish to understand what is Freud's true preoccupation as the function of fantasm is revealed to him, remember the development, which is so central for us, of the *Wolf Man*. He applies himself, in a way that can almost be described as anguish, to the question—what is the first encounter, the real that lies behind the phantasy?"[32] Lacan

". . . the phantasy is never anything more than the screen that conceals something quite **primary**, something determinant in the function of repetition."[33] Lacan

*

---

31. *Four Fundamental Concepts*, 40.

32. *Four Fundamental Concepts*, 54.

33. *Four Fundamental Concepts*, 60.

Nasio

THERE IS NO REPETITION WITHOUT A CONSCIOUSNESS THAT
COUNTS THE NUMBER OF TIMES AN EVENT IS REPEATED.

This is an excerpt from our book, Introduction à la Topologie
de Lacan *where we recall the necessity of a consciousness that
counts the successive occurrences of repetition.*

The minimal unity of the repetitive movement is involves a *progres-sive* vector, and another *retroactive* vector. The progressive vector, A→ B, reveals the two states of an event: first, before being repeated, A; then when it is repeated, B (see figure 1). Now, we cannot address repetition without introducing a trivial, but decisive, third element: the simple fact of **counting**. If we did not count a before and an after, or rather a first, a second, and an umpteenth time, there would never be repetition. In other words,

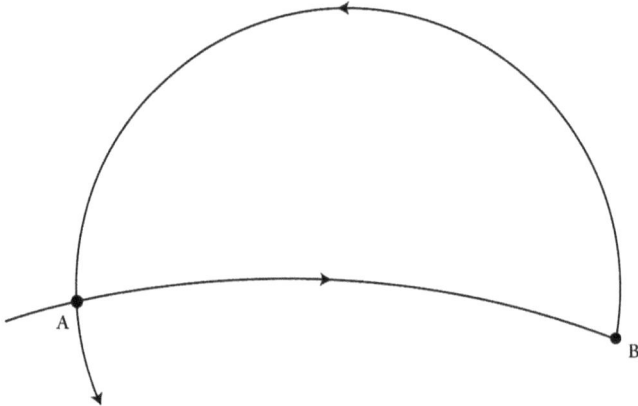

Figure 1. Schema of deferred action.

the state of the event before being repeated becomes the repeated state on the condition that someone counts; understanding that the count is only verified once the repetition is accomplished in B. Before the repetition and consequently before the counting, A does not exist as first; A will only be first if a second, B, repeats it. We must then trace the vector B → A retroactively, and thus signify that retroactively B determines A as an original event. This first loop schematizes the movement that we know as deferred action [*après coup*]. **A** only becomes deferred affect, after we have counted **B** as its repetition.

If now we note figure 2, the large loop surrounding the small loop represents the very operation of counting, or more precisely, the element that makes calculus possible, namely, writing. That element—writing—indispensable to the constitution of series of numbers is not, however, itself reducible to a number. It is outside of the series, or, outside of repetitive succession. It is as something external that bears the name that was given by Lacan: *Un-en-plus* [One-in-excess].

We have said that with respect to the horizon of counting, that there is always someone who counts and calculates, but who counts or calculates without being able to count itself. The radical powerlessness of the being who speaks and undergoes jouissance is that of not being able to recognize itself in successive repetitions. The subject counts, but does not count itself, or it is counted as a subject minus one [*en moins*]. The final looping of this double curve signifies that repetition is accomplished and takes place with the birth of the new subject that we just identified as a subject minus one. The point C in figure 2 indicates three things: the closure of the movement of repetition, the closure of the operation of counting and engendering a new subject, the subject of the unconscious."[34]

---

34. J.-D. Nasio, *Introduction à la Topologie de Lacan* (Paris: Payot, 2010), 85–88.

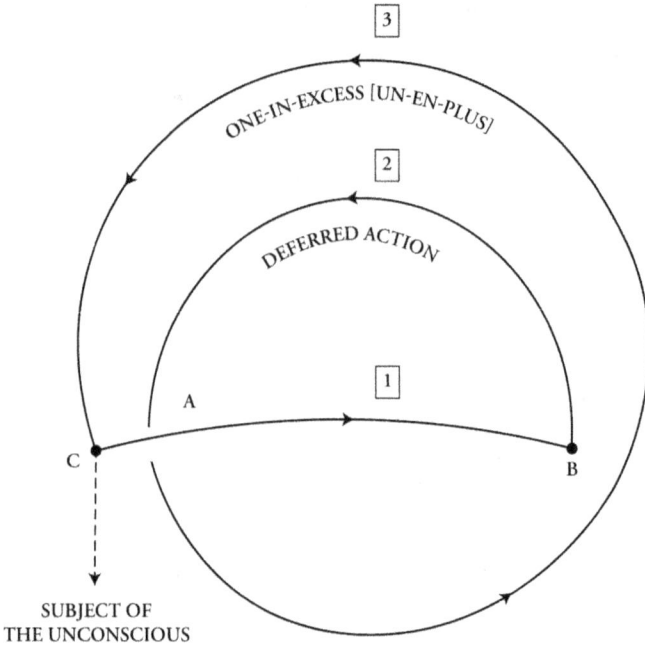

Figure 2. Engendering the subject of the unconscious at the point of closure, C, of the repetitive loop.

Index

www.ingramcontent.com/pod-product-compliance
Lightning Source LLC
Chambersburg PA
CBHW020358270326
41926CB00007B/492